# Awaking
## THE GOD
## within

Learning to Partner With God
to Create a Life You Love

OWL IN THE
juniper

Cover by Monica Woolley
Graphic Design by Monica Woolley

Edited by Mary Scoresby

ISBN 979-8-9880607-0-3 (paperback)
ISBN 979-8-9880607-1-0 (eBook)

Library of Congress Control Number: 2023906220

First edition


Publisher's Cataloging-in-Publication
(Provided by Cassidy Cataloguing Services, Inc.)

    Names:
    Bangerter, Lacey Woolley,1986- author. | Nesbit, Rebecca Ann, 1975- author.

    Title:
    Awaking the God within : learning to partner with God to create a life you love / by Lacey Woolley Bangerter and Rebecca Ann Nesbit, Ph.D.

    Description:
    First edition. | [Athens, Georgia] : Owl in the Juniper Publishing, [2023] | Includes bibliographical references.

    Identifiers:
    ISBN: 979-8-9880607-0-3 (paperback) | 979-8-9880607-1-0 (eBook) | LCCN: 2023906220

    Subjects:
    LCSH: God (Christianity)--Knowableness. | Spiritual life--Christianity. | Self-actualization (Psychology) | Self-realization. | Stress management. | Agent (Philosophy) | Cognitive balance--Religious aspects. | Attitude (Psychology) | Change (Psychology) | Conduct of life. | LCGFT: Self-help publications. | BISAC: SELF-HELP / Personal Growth / General. | SELF-HELP / Spiritual.

    Classification:
    LCC: BF637.S4 B36 2023 | DDC: 158.1--dc23


Published by Owl in the Juniper Publishing
owlinthejuniperpublishing@gmail.com

# Awaking THE GOD within

### Learning to Partner With God to Create a Life You Love

## By Lacey Woolley Bangerter and Rebecca Ann Nesbit, Ph.D.

# Table of Contents

# Introduction

God is the Master Creator; as a child of God, your destiny is to become a powerful, master creator like God. The purpose of this book is to help you to awaken and use your own God-given, creative power to create what you desire in life. This book will help you to become more deeply aware of who you really are—your true, eternal, divine self—and of how powerful you are. You will learn how to use your personal power more effectively, particularly by choosing to connect with God and allowing God's power to flow into your life. This book will show you how to be in a balanced state with God so that you can fully access God's power and grace, add it to your own personal power, and learn to create your desires.

You are likely familiar with many of the concepts that we discuss in this book: repentance, forgiveness, faith, hope, and charity. However, this book will help you to understand these principles in a deeper, more powerful way. You will come to see them as important tools of creation that help you to allow God's help in your life. You

will understand that hope, faith, and charity are a God-given pattern for learning how to become a master creator. At the end of this book, you will understand hope, faith, and charity in an entirely new way.

If you desire to improve some aspect of your life, then this book is for you! You may be trying to live of a life of faith and hope by doing all of the things you think God wants you to do, but often feel overwhelmed and stressed. Worse yet, you might feel stuck in a life of pain and struggle. You might feel some disappointment in how your life is going. You might wonder if you can really receive what you desire from God. If you desire to break that cycle and live the life of joy that God desires for you, then this book will be an important part of your journey.

This book is about personal development. However, unlike most books on personal development, this book has an integral and intentional focus on God and Jesus Christ. We desire to teach you how to deepen your relationship with God and Christ. While this book might particularly resonate with Christians, anyone who believes in a Higher Power will be able to apply these principles and tools to their life and reap the benefits.

Our religious background is in The Church of Jesus Christ of Latter-day Saints. We share this with you so that you know the cultural and doctrinal frame of reference for this book. We occasionally share scriptures from the Bible and other scriptural works unique to our church called The Book of Mormon and the Doctrine and Covenants. Even if this is not your religion or faith tradition, we believe these inspired words will benefit you and help you to understand the concepts in this book. As you read this book, we invite you to seek to be taught by God—or your

Higher Power—so that you can gain the insights intended for you. We emphasize that the ideas and truths shared in this book transcend the boundaries of any church or religion. Anyone who desires a better, more joyful life can use and apply these principles to learn how to create.

We invite you to have an open mind and heart as you read this book. This book is about your personal journey with God, so we encourage you to invite God to be with you as you read. Pray about the book's content so that you will know what you need to learn and understand from this book. God will show you how to apply these truths in your life.

We are grateful that you have decided to read this book. We have written this book to give more people access to these powerful ideas and tools that have blessed our lives so much. Our desire is to empower others to walk in faith with God and to live more joyfully. We would like to share more about ourselves and how we came to collaborate on this project.

# Lacey's Story

As a child, I quickly learned that I was different from other people. While most people could not sense what was happening in the spiritual realm, I could see and perceive the spirits around me. As a child, it was difficult to make sense of and understand my experiences with these spirits because no one around me had the same gift that I did. Unfortunately, many of my childhood experiences were with dark spirits. I remember one evening as I was falling asleep, the room around me got very dark. I could see a dark form standing over my bed and felt a menacing spirit. It bent over until it was above my face and told me that I would never be able to escape it. I was terrified. I could not move or speak. After taunting me for a while, the spirit finally left, and I was able to move again. That experience traumatized me because I was so afraid of the spirit coming back. When I told my mother about my experience, she told me that I needed to live righteously so that these evil spirits would not have power over me.

I took that to heart. I believed that the way to stay safe from the evil spirits that were haunting me was to be as close to God as possible. I spent the next decade trying to do just that—to live as perfectly and righteously as I could so that God would protect me from the evil spirits. I bought religious posters to hang on the walls of my room. I played religious and classical music all of the time, particularly before going to bed. I would even sleep with my scriptures in my arms so that I would be protected from the terrorizing evil spirits at night. When I was 15, I went a year without watching a single movie with any degrading material in it. I was determined to stay as close to God as possible by doing all the "right" things—everything I had been taught that God wanted me to do.

I lived as strictly as I could because I was afraid that if I did even one wrong thing, God would not protect me. I was doing everything I could to try to please God and earn His help. I was so strict and hard on myself for every little mistake that after a decade, I reached my breaking point. I just couldn't do it anymore. It was too stressful, and I felt like I would never be able to do enough to get God's help. Besides that, my efforts were not working. Despite my very best efforts to live righteously, I was still experiencing trauma from evil spirits and living in fear. God hadn't shown up for me in the way I hoped He would.

I still tried to live a good life, but I told God that I was done trying to do everything perfectly. I was tired of being afraid and worrying that doing one little negative thing would invite evil spirits into my life. I was just over it. I started to distance myself from God because I believed that God was indifferent to me. I had tried so hard to be good, but God didn't protect me. Why didn't He do more

for me? What more did God want from me? I wondered if maybe I just wasn't worthy of God's help. Maybe I would never be worthy enough to receive it. I felt that God had let me down.

One night in 2007 while I was going to sleep, I had another experience with the spirit realm, but one that was completely opposite to my prior experiences. The spirit of my great-grandfather came to visit me. He told me that he was frequently there with me, watching over me. His moment with me was short, but it helped me realize that if I could perceive the negative and evil in the spiritual realm, I could also perceive the good and the light. I knew that I had some kind of spiritual gift, and—even though I was scared of it—I wanted to learn how to use it for good. I desired to learn how to do so and prayed for help to develop this gift.

This increased my desire to be close to God. However, instead of turning to God out of fear, I turned to God out of joy and peace. I wasn't thinking about trying to be perfect to get something from God. I was excited about what God could teach me, and I allowed God to lead me on a journey of discovery. This journey wasn't easy because it showed me that much of what I had been taught about God was incomplete or incorrect and didn't represent who God is or my real relationship with Him. I had to work hard to let go of these deep-rooted cultural patterns. A mentor came into my life, and she taught me how to repent by visualizing Jesus Christ standing in front of me, willing to take whatever I desired to give to Him. This opened me up to profound healing. Every time I repented, I received more truth from God. My relationship with God started to flourish, and I began to know Him in ways I never thought

possible. I felt so chummy with Him. I began to know that I was His daughter and that He delighted in me just being me. It was a huge relief to give up the belief that I had to prove my righteousness to God in order to receive anything from Him. I was finding more joy in my life and learning more about what I wanted for myself. These new discoveries were exciting to me and filled me with a new sense of life.

I began to have a desire to teach others how to transform their lives as mine had been transformed, but I didn't have the confidence to put myself out there. I didn't believe that others would find me worth listening to. Then in 2015, I was at an activity with several women playing a "get to know you" game which consisted of answering random questions if a ball was thrown to you. The ball was thrown to me and I had to answer this question: "What do you want to be when you grow up?" I told the group that I wanted to be a motivational speaker. A friend sitting next to me chuckled and said, "I can actually see that!" Laughing with her, I again started to dismiss this idea, but I couldn't quite let it go.

Over the next couple months, I pondered that desire. My pondering brought up my insecurities and confidence issues, and I had to spend some time working through those feelings. By early 2016, I could not resist the pull any longer, so I finally confided my desire to my husband. He quickly let me know that if I really wanted it, then he would support it—as he always has done with any of my desires. It felt so good to voice this desire to another human being in a sincere and genuine way. I had always believed that there was something wrong or bad about voicing my own desires, so this was a huge step for me.

Saying it aloud made me think that maybe, just maybe, this could possibly happen.

My desire continued to grow over the next month, so I finally decided to share my desire aloud to God. I did so, and then held my breath. It felt pretty bold to be telling God what I wanted, but I was immediately filled with peace and love. I knew that God had heard my prayer and that He was on board with my desire. In a joking way I told Him, "Well, I guess if this is going to happen, I'm going to need a message to motivate the world with!"

Six months later, my husband and I had moved from our townhouse to a small condo as we waited for our new home to be built. While in this transitory state, an idea came to me. It wasn't a big idea at first, but I felt that I needed to pay attention to what was coming to my mind. I started to make notes and to talk to family members about the ideas so that I could practice explaining them. It took me a few months to get all of my ideas out on paper and organized. As I did so, I started seeing how the patterns, formulas, and concepts that were coming to me related to doctrines and truths that I had been taught at church. Many of the principles and concepts that I had been taught, such as faith, hope, charity, repentance, forgiveness, and the Sabbath day were abstract; they were difficult to understand and even more difficult to apply on a daily basis. These concepts now started to unfold for me, and I understood them in a simplified way that allowed me to apply and practice them. I saw how these truths had helped transform my life, and I felt even more joy as I started to live these truths on a daily basis.

My head felt like a university with all the information that was coming to me. I started to call them my daily

downloads from God. As I applied these concepts, my life became easy, peaceful, joyful, and full of love—and I *do not* use those words lightly. I really felt those beautiful emotions and lived with them daily—and still do to this day. When the downloads started to slow down, I felt a great desire to organize them and help others learn how to apply faith, hope, charity, repentance, and other powerful spiritual concepts to their lives. I desired to simplify these concepts for others. I wanted to help others learn how to be more of a friend with God and to walk completely yoked with Him in ease. I wrote down all of these ideas and organized them as best as I could. As I came to the end of my first draft, I had a quiet, peaceful moment with God that let me know: "Here is the message you wanted!" I broke down and cried because I was filled with gratitude. I had prayed for a message to share with the world, and God delivered a more profound message than I ever could have learned from any other source.

I started sharing this message with others and taught classes about how to use faith, hope, and charity to create their greatest desires. After a few years of teaching, I started to feel that I needed to write this all down in a book, but I needed help to do so. I shared my desire with God, and that is when I met Becky.

# Becky's Story

In January 2013, I remember getting out of the shower, running a comb through my hair, and seeing a large wad of hair on the comb. It was very distressing, especially since it was not the first time that had happened. I knew that my hair was falling out because I was living with constant, overwhelming stress—and had been for years. Stress was taking other tolls on my body. I was also rapidly gaining weight, getting sick almost every month, experiencing extreme insomnia, and grinding my teeth. The stress was all due to my drive to be successful at work, to be perfect in my observance of church standards and service, and my perfectionistic approach to my personal goals. I wanted to be perfect at everything, and I wanted to live up to everyone's (and my own) expectations. I believed that the way to be loved and accepted—and the way to receive God's help and blessings—was to be as perfect as humanly possible. The time demands of these pursuits often caused me to withdraw from friends and family, which led to feelings of loneliness and isolation. That day in my bathroom, I

knew that if I didn't get the stress under control, it would destroy my body and my life.

I began to feel there was something wrong with my approach to life. I was doing all of the "right" things—all of the things that I had been taught to do—but I was unhappy and unfulfilled. Years of unhappiness were taking their toll on me, and I was angry at God. I had been taught that if I did all the right things—was kind and compassionate, served others, kept the commandments, went to church, prayed and read scriptures, used my time productively—that I would be happy. If that were true, then why was I so unhappy even after years of doing those things? I would listen to people at church talk about how to be happy, and they always seemed to say that the secret to happiness was just doing more and being better. At that point in my life, I didn't see any possible way that I could do more or be better. It would be like squeezing blood from a rock. My body was literally falling apart from years of trying to do more and be better, so I knew that was not the answer. It couldn't be the answer because that answer was literally destroying my body. There was something that I was missing—something that I didn't understand about having a happy life.

Even my closest friends and family members had no idea of the depth of my sadness and pain; to most people, my life looked pretty good. I had received my Ph.D. and was working as a professor at a university. I was excelling in all aspects of my work and made a name for myself in that arena. I had many opportunities to travel and have new experiences, including visiting more than 20 countries (at that time). I was very talented and involved in many different activities and groups. I served in many

leadership positions at work and church. People respected and admired me; many thought that my life was blessed. But even with all of that, I was struggling enormously.

There were two specific personal issues that had plagued me my whole life. The first was my weight; by the world's standards I was (and still am) morbidly obese. I had been overweight since I was a child and could never seem to achieve—let alone maintain—a healthy weight. Even after years of exercising and dieting, my weight would constantly fluctuate. When I would have success at losing weight, I would inevitably end up gaining it back. What is worse, my weight had taken a huge emotional toll on me since I was in kindergarten. I was bullied in school because of my body, and I often felt insecure and rejected. Decades later, I was still dealing with issues of body image, self-acceptance, and all of the insecurity and pain that come from being an overweight woman in a world that values and praises the opposite.

My second struggle was being single. I had always wanted to find a good man to marry and to have a family with. I wanted someone to love—and someone who would love me. Between being a naturally shy person (which I could hide in most contexts) and my body image issues, I was awkward and insecure in the dating arena. That translated into a lot of pain around dating. For years, I worked on trying to make myself more attractive in the dating market. I thought that if I could just figure out what was wrong with me and fix it, then I would find someone to date. But my efforts didn't avail me any success. I had few first dates and no second dates; I was rejected constantly. I just couldn't find someone to date, and I no longer even

believed that it was possible. My situation felt hopeless, and I wondered if I even deserved to have romantic love.

No matter what I did, I could not seem to come to any kind of peace regarding my weight or my relationship status. I felt worthless and unlovable. No wonder I buried myself in accomplishments at work and at church. I had to escape the pain somehow. I had to do something to prove that I had some worth.

In January 2013 when I had that experience of getting out the shower and seeing my hair fall out, I turned 38 years old and I was desperate. I needed answers and I needed solutions—real solutions. I prayed very earnestly for help and instruction. I prayed to understand how I could live a happy life without all of the stress and pressure that were overwhelming me. Shortly thereafter, a friend asked me to go with her to attend a weekly class on mindfulness that was being taught at the local university. I agreed to do so, and that class started to open my eyes. I started learning some principles that had been foreign to my way of living. For example, I learned that people who have more self-compassion actually do better at accomplishing their goals compared to people (like me) who just beat themselves up all of the time. I also learned about tools like meditation and visualization that are helpful in reducing stress. That class started me on a journey of learning and discovery.

I started reading more and taking more classes. While I had always read a lot of personal development books, they were often about topics like time management—books that would help me to learn how to do more. Now I was reading more about mindfulness, meditation, and other spiritual topics. I also listened to webinars and

participated in online classes about a range of topics, such as radical forgiveness, chakra healing, feng shui, meditation, the law of attraction, and a host of other related topics. God's answer to my prayer was to lead me to seek for more answers outside of the religious box that I had grown up in—and that was an answer that surprised me. But it began a marvelous journey. I exposed myself to a greater range of teachers and ideas that started to really deepen my understanding of Christ's teachings and the religious principles that I had been taught. I finally felt like I understood more about faith, surrender, and the power of love. I was excited about finding new meaning in the scriptures because of what I was learning from these other sources. Because of my willingness to follow God's direction and learn from variety of other sources, the concepts that I had learned at church were now making sense at a deeper level.

I learned several important truths through this process. First, I learned that "doing more" and "being better" are *not* the answer! So many of the obligations that I was trapped in were driven by my fear of what others would think of me if I didn't do everything and do it perfectly. I learned that those were not God's expectations or desires for me. I learned techniques to help me to let go of that fear and to embrace more of what I wanted for myself and my life. I came to understand the power of limiting beliefs and the importance of my mind in shaping my world and creating my reality. Even better, I started to learn how to change and shape those beliefs. I learned about the importance of emotions and emotional healing. Most importantly, I learned about true surrender and how to really work with Jesus Christ to release my mental and emotional baggage.

My friends and family members started to notice that I was happier and freer. The changes happening in my life were noticeable to everyone around me. Even now, I am learning a new way to live—one that is based in my heart and my relationship with God, not on other people's expectations for me. I now have a wonderful boyfriend who loves me greatly and brings so much sweetness into my life. I am still overweight, but I am learning to love and accept my body as it is. I trust that when I am done learning from this body, the weight will change naturally on its own. Every day, Jesus Christ heals more of the pain from my past. Many things in my life are getting easier and work out better for me. Many days when I pray, I cry tears of gratitude for how good my life is and for how far I have come from that day in 2013. When I look into my future, I see hope, wonder, and excitement about the things to come. I trust that the joy, peace, and love in my life will continue to grow.

In 2019, my mom shared with me some of Lacey's podcasts and other materials that she had posted on her website. I really appreciated what I heard in those podcasts because what Lacey taught fit so well with other things that I had been learning in my healing journey. I appreciated that Lacey helped me to connect what I was discovering back to truths that I had learned—but never fully understood—at church. In early 2020, I decided to take a weekly online class from Lacey about finding balance with God and creating what you desire. I enjoyed the class tremendously, and the things Lacey taught resonated with me. It all resonated deeply with me. At the end of the class, Lacey mentioned that she was looking for someone to help her turn the course material into a book.

I had been thinking of writing a book, so I jumped at the opportunity.

Throughout the intervening two and half years, Lacey and I have worked hard to get this book ready for publication. Throughout the whole process, I have had to apply the tools in this book to overcome the fears, insecurities, and obstacles that were holding me back. Along with that, I have continued to seek other opportunities for learning and healing. A couple years earlier, a few of my friends had started a nonprofit focused on a Christ-based approach to emotional and spiritual healing called One Heart One Light (www.oneheartonelight.org). In 2021, One Heart One Light started hosting women's healing retreats, and I attended the first one. Everything that I learned and experienced at the retreat fit so well with the lessons and tools that we were writing in this book. It amazes me how hard God is working to get this information out to people, to help people to heal from the past, and to inspire them to embrace a brighter future.

# Book Overview

This book starts with a chapter about agency—a foundational principle for taking ownership of *your* life and stepping into your power so that you can become a master creator. The book is then divided into two major sections. In the first section, we discuss the concept of being in balance with God—a state where you are emotionally peaceful and allow God to work in your life. In this section, we define what balance is and discuss why it is important, especially for the creation process. We also share how to get into balance with God. This section covers repentance and forgiveness in detail because they are two important tools to help you to achieve and maintain balance. The second section of the book discusses the creation process. We discuss how hope, faith, and charity are the perfect framework for creation. We discuss in detail how each of these three spiritual concepts can be used as tools to help you to create what you desire. We conclude by sharing how resting in God can help you to receive what you desire.

While we hope that you will learn many new truths and principles throughout this book, our primary focus is teaching you how to make these truths work in your life. Our goal is that you understand these concepts and know how to apply them so that when you are finished with this book, you will feel empowered to use these tools and techniques to reclaim your agency, to connect with God's power, and to see miracles happen in your life.

# Chapter 1
## Awaking Your Agency

We will emphasize many times throughout this book that God desires for you to become a master creator—just as He is! In order to become a master creator, you will need to learn to access and rely upon God's power in your life. We will discuss how to do this in the following chapters. But it takes more than God's power for all of this to happen. *Your* power is an important part of the equation. Yes, God is all-powerful and can do anything. But in order for God to help you become a master creator, you must first be willing and able to ignite your personal power by awakening your agency.

This is why agency is important; creation is as much about your power as it is about God's power. Partnering with God requires you to awaken your power, which means that you need to understand what your agency is and how to use it. By taking full responsibility for your agency and being intentional about your choices, you will be a more successful creator. You will be able to meet God at the point where your power and God's power arc the

greatest, and that will bring miracles into your life. This chapter discusses what agency is, how it plays out in your daily life, and ways that you might be neglecting to use your agency. This understanding will help you to own your agency –to awaken your personal power—rather than give it away to others.

## What Is Agency?

You were endowed with agency from the moment your spirit started to exist.[1] Agency is not just a right or a privilege. It is not just a gift. It is part of who you are. You have never been without it, and you will always have it.

Most people describe agency as the ability to choose, but agency is much more than choice. It is power. We define agency as follows:

> *Agency = the activation power; the power to activate or initiate the process of spiritual creation*

Everything that you experience on Earth was created spiritually before it was created physically. God modeled this pattern when the Earth was created. "For I, the Lord God, created all things of which I have spoken, spiritually, before they were naturally upon the face of the earth" (Moses 3:5). If you desire to create something on Earth, you must follow God's pattern and first create it spiritually. In fact, everything that you desire to have, receive, or become must be created spiritually before it will come into existence physically. Agency is crucial in this process because it initiates the spiritual creation of your desire.

---

[1] "The Lord said unto Enoch: Behold these thy brethren; they are the workmanship of mine own hands, and I gave unto them their knowledge, in the day I created them; and in the Garden of Eden, gave I unto man his agency" Moses 7:32

The moment you make a choice, your agency—your power—activates everything around it. It immediately begins to organize matter, elements, and energy into your chosen desire. This process happens no matter what your choice is, without regard for whether that choice is "right" or "wrong," "good" or "bad." The power of agency will commence spiritual creation. If that spiritual creation is sustained, it will eventually become a physical creation—something you can experience with your physical body.

Agency can activate spiritual creation, but it cannot sustain it. When you make a choice, your agency sets the wheels in motion, but in order for that creation to manifest in your physical life, it must be sustained by another power. The optimal sustaining power is love; love can give life to your desires. When a choice is not fueled by love, there is not enough sustaining power for it to manifest in a physical form or for it to have a long life in the physical plane. Without love, the spiritual matter that you activated dissipates and returns to its original state. Your choice did not have the sustaining power.

We use the analogy of a match to clarify these ideas. Suppose you are camping in the mountains and you are hungry and cold. You desire warmth and light; that is your choice. You lay out your firewood and grab a match. When you strike the match, it ignites a tiny fire. By coming into contact with the wood, the fire grows and becomes brighter and stronger. As long as the fire has enough wood, it will continue to burn and provide you with your desire—warmth and light. To receive your desired state, you need both the match and the fuel to create and sustain a fire. The match created the initial spark for the fire, and the fuel allowed the fire to grow and survive.

Agency is like the match. It is the activation power. It creates the initial spark of your choice—the thing that you desire. It gets the whole process started and heading in the right direction. When that activation power is coupled with the right fuel, your desire can grow and be sustained until you achieve your desired state. Both the activation power and the sustaining power are necessary for creation. In part two, we will discuss more about how to fuel your creation process with the perfect fuel—charity. Our focus in this chapter is to help you to understand the important role of agency in the creation process. Just by making a choice, you unleash a tremendous amount of creative power to work on your behalf.

## Agency in Your Daily Life

You use your agency throughout the whole day; you are continually making choices about what you desire to do or experience. Sometimes using your agency leads to an immediate, tangible outcome. For example, you might be hungry and desire to eat. When you choose to eat, your body is instantly on the way to the kitchen to make something to eat. As soon as you had the thought, you could direct your body to take the actions necessary to fulfill your desire for food. Throughout the day, you have many simple desires that are easily met with some small action on your part. When your choice is directly linked to a physical action, the link between spiritual creation and physical creation is clear, direct, and immediate. In those cases, your agency activates your physical body to take action.

However, many of your desires are more complex, particularly those desires pertaining to the type of life you wish to experience. If your desire pertains to a state of

being that you wish to achieve, then the link between spiritual creation and physical creation might not be as immediate, clear, and tangible as going to the kitchen to make a piece of toast. For example, you might desire to get a better job. The moment you choose to seek a better job, your agency activates the spiritual creation of what you desire. It starts moving all of the elements and matter in the direction of your choice and starts opening up the path to a better job. If you continue to fuel this desire using the creation tools in part two, then you will notice that things start to happen. Perhaps a friend calls you to tell you about a job opportunity at his sister's company. Maybe you attend a networking event and meet someone who feels that you would be perfect for an open position at her agency. Your boss might decide to give you the promotion that you have been asking for. You made the choice about what you desired to experience and that set spiritual creation in motion. When that desire is also sustained by love, things will start to happen in your life, and God can deliver your desire to you.

## Your Agency Is Always Active

At this point, you might be thinking to yourself that you have known several people who desired a better job and never received it. Or you may be thinking to yourself: "There are plenty of times that I have desired something, and it didn't happen. Just because I choose something doesn't mean I will get it." Yes, that may have been true of your past experience, but it does not have to be true of your future.

Your agency is always active, whether you are conscious of it or not. Sometimes you use your agency to unintentionally create things that you do not truly desire. Fear

is also a sustaining power that can bring your spiritual creations into fruition in the physical world. The problem is that creations made from fear tend to get distorted in the process. Sometimes your creations get so warped that they arrive as the exact opposite of what you desire. If you desire a better career, but you fuel that choice with fear instead of love, then you probably will not receive your desired outcome—a better career. It is possible that your fear can even cause your situation at work to get worse. Instead of picturing what you desired and fueling that creation with love, you focused on your current situation and kept re-creating it out of fear.

Agency activates spiritual creation regardless of the content of the choice you make. All choices bring a range of consequences with them, and you might label those consequences as being either good or bad depending on how they affect you and how they make you feel. But the power itself—agency—is a neutral power. It applies to any choice, any creation, any desired outcome. The more you learn about the creation process, your tools of creation, and how to bring God's power into the process, the more you will be able to create what you desire and avoid creating what you do not desire. Greater understanding will allow you to be intentional about what you are creating in your life.

No matter what your past experiences have been or what frustrations you have experienced over unmet desires, our invitation to you is to open yourself up to something new—a new way to live and to be. Throughout this book, we will teach you how you can nurture your desired spiritual creations into your physical reality and how to avoid creating from fear. The first step in that process is

to recognize that you are filled with creative power, that your agency is what starts the creation process, and that you are always using your agency whether you are aware of it or not.

## Giving Your Agency Away

Your agency can never be taken from you. It is your inherent power. However, you might give your agency away to others rather than fully claiming it for yourself. Your agency is intended to help you to create what you desire. You give your agency away when you allow other people or institutions to make your choices for you, rather than listening to what is in your heart and what you truly desire. For example, maybe your family owns a restaurant and runs it as a family business. They want you to take it over next year when your father retires. But you don't really want to be in the restaurant business because you don't really enjoy that work. You would rather go to school to be an engineer. If you choose to run the family business to keep your family happy rather than pursue your own desired career, then you have given your agency away to your family. They chose your career for you rather than you choosing it for yourself. Your family has directed your creative power instead of you directing it.

This is a typical scenario if you are a people pleaser and you feel that you have to make certain decisions in order to make other people happy, even if those choices do not make you happy. That is a misuse of your agency. The purpose of your agency is to bring *you* joy! God creates because His creations bring Him joy. God desires the same thing for you. Your power to create is greatest when the thought of what you are creating fills you with joy. This does not mean that you can never compromise with other

people or that you cannot do things for others. What it does mean is that you will benefit by becoming aware of whether you are making your choices to please yourself or to please other people. Living to keep other people happy will not help you become a master creator. You might have been doing this for so long that you don't even know which choices will make you happy. Being out of touch with what you truly desire and what truly brings you joy is a recipe for giving your agency away.

You might also give your agency away to the norms, values, and customs of your society, religion, culture, or generation. You might consider yourself a rule follower who follows all of the spoken and unspoken rules governing a particular situation. For example, your culture might dictate that women do not enter certain careers, like air traffic control. If you are a woman and the desire of your heart is to be an air traffic controller, but you shy away from that career because of gender norms, then you have given your agency away to your culture. We are not saying that you can never follow any norms, rules, or laws or that you should make it a point to openly defy them. We are saying that you will benefit by being aware of situations when societal or cultural rules conflict with choices that would bring joy to your heart. In those instances, you might want to break a rule in order to create what you desire for your life.

Devout, religious people sometimes give their agency away to God's commandments. We are not saying that God's commandments are not important. Commandments are valuable guides in life. However, there is a big difference between obeying a commandment because it is what you desire to do and obeying a commandment because you

are afraid of the consequences of not doing so. It could be fear of punishment from God or fear that you will not receive blessings from God. It could just be fear of what other people will think and how they will judge you for ignoring that commandment. It comes down to your motivation and your desire. When you choose to obey a commandment out of fear, then you have given your agency away. When you choose to obey a commandment because it is what you desire to do, you are using your agency.

Remember, God is the Master Creator and desires that you become a master creator as well. The only way to master the creation process is to awaken your agency, your own creative power. It is important that you stop giving your agency away to other people. Reclaim your agency. You can identify situations in your life where you have given away your agency by identifying what makes you angry. Just begin to notice the situations in your life where you take action to please others but feel a little bit of anger about it. That anger is built up resentment at yourself for letting your boundaries be crossed and not making a choice that would serve you better or honor your own boundaries. Those situations are good places to start making new choices—choices that honor your agency.

## Giving Your Agency to God

There are many scenarios where you might surrender your agency to God. You might try to let God make your choices for you. For example, you might be considering several different universities to attend. You visit each one and make a list of the pros and cons of attending each one. Then you pray and ask God to tell you where to attend school. That is giving your agency to God. God desires that you choose for yourself what university to attend and

then seek confirmation for that choice. Instead of asking God to choose for you, tell God what you hope to experience at school and how you would like to learn and grow. Tell God that you think this school will provide that for you and that you want to know if there is a better option for you to pursue. God desires to give you direction so you can find out what is best for *you*. You will hear that direction much more clearly when you are using your agency rather than giving it away.

At this point, you might be thinking to yourself that we are totally off base, that you are always supposed to defer your desires to God. At church, you have often heard the phrase "God's will be done"[2]—and you might even say that yourself. The contextual meaning of "will" in this phrase is "something desired."[3] The phrase "God's will be done" implies that your desires are secondary to God's desires. It implies that you need to give your agency to God and let Him choose for you. It also implies that you must use your agency and creative power in subjugation to God's desires. That is not the case. We assert that it is a misunderstanding of God's desires for you.

God does not desire to make your choices for you. In fact, God *will not* make your choices for you because God *will never* violate the law of agency. You chose to come into this world so that you could learn through the experience of making choices in this environment. God desires that you choose what you desire and then partner with Him to help you create it. God is a loving parent who wants you to

---

[2] See Luke 22:42

[3] Merriam-Webster defines "will" (noun) as "something desired, especially a choice or determination of one having authority or power."
(https://www.merriam-webster.com/dictionary/will)

become a god or goddess yourself. You cannot become like God unless you learn how to fully embrace your agency and learn how to create things—first spiritually, then physically. In order for God to bless your life with miracles and abundance, you need to be actively involved through the full use of your agency. As long as you are giving your agency to God and wanting God to make your choices for you, you limit God's power in your life and you limit your ability to create.

Surrendering your will to God is not about giving up your desires, but about allowing God to bring you those desires in His way. Surrendering your will to God does not mean that you surrender the choice; it means that you surrender the exact circumstances and method by which that choice is manifested in the physical realm. God desires—and expects—you to choose the end goal, the "what." He merely wants you to surrender the "how" to Him. Surrendering to God means that you do not try to force your desired state into existence, but that you instead allow God to lead you to it. Surrendering is about letting go of micromanaging the process and leaving it to God. But first you choose the direction that you desire. God's will is about the process; your will is about the desired outcome.

God's will, or desire, for you is that you use your agency to lay hold of all of the beautiful gifts and blessings that God can possibly give you. "Behold, this is my will; ask and ye shall receive; but men do not always do my will" (Doctrine and Covenants 103:31). God said it right there. His will is for you to ask for what you desire—your choice. God delights in blessing you with your desires and wants you to believe that you can receive them. In order

for your desires to come into existence in your physical reality, you need the sustaining power of love. You will only be able to generate enough love to fuel your creations if you truly love the desired outcome. You will only love an outcome that is truly your own desire—not someone else's, not even God's. God knows that He cannot really teach you to create unless you are creating something that *you* desire to create. You must be willing to choose what you desire as part of this process.

## Are You Giving Your Agency Away?

You might also give your agency away to your own fears. You may be afraid of what other people will say or do if you make a particular choice. Or you may just be afraid of a wrong or bad decision, meaning a decision that might bring you undesirable consequences. For example, imagine you are retiring and trying to decide where you want to buy a home and live the rest of your life. You might be so worried about making a wrong decision that you keep postponing making the choice. Or you might choose where to live but feel anxious about whether you made the right choice. You become preoccupied with fear and second-guessing yourself.

When you are tempted to give your agency away to fear, remember Jesus Christ. Remember that He stands in the role of your Savior. "For God sent not his Son into the world to condemn the world; but that the world through him might be saved" (John 3:17). Jesus Christ is there to rescue and save you when you regret a choice you have made. The whole purpose of having a Savior is so that you can make choices without fear. You are here on the earth to learn and grow through the use of your agency, and God knew that many things you would choose would be

things that could cause you or others pain. All of the consequences of your decisions can be healed through Jesus Christ's power. Essentially, you can make as many mistakes as you desire. You can make as many mistakes as you need to in order to have the experiences you choose and to grow in the ways that you desire to grow. Do not be afraid of your own agency. Do not be afraid of making choices. Do not be afraid of the consequences of your choices; God will help you to navigate those. If you truly want to activate your agency and take control of that power, then you need to stop being afraid of your own decisions.

This is a good point to stop and ask yourself how you are doing at claiming and using your own agency. Be honest with yourself.

- Where in your life do you compromise your agency?

- What choices do you make because you think they are expected of you rather than being something that you truly desire for yourself?

- Where in your life do you try to get God to make your choices for you?

- What choices are you afraid of making?

Take a moment to tune into your heart and ask where in your life you are giving your agency away. You can choose today to reclaim your agency and to choose what you desire—just as Lacey did in the following story.

## Lacey's Story About Her Red Dress

Once a year, my husband's work hosts a fancy awards banquet. We had attended the event the previous year and enjoyed it, but this time I wanted a fancy new dress to

wear to the banquet. While it might seem like a frivo-lous or materialistic desire, I had learned that the creation process works best when you are using it to create some-thing you actually want—not what others tell you to want. I didn't want to give my agency away to others by judging my own desire as frivolous, materialistic, or unimportant.

I used my agency to tell God what I wanted. I told God I wanted a dress that fit me perfectly, that I felt beauti-ful in, that others (especially my husband) would think was stunning, and that fit our budget. As I was praying, I started to feel really excited about my dress. I even told God how much I loved that I could come tell Him about a dress I wanted. I felt that God shared my excitement and joy. I knew that God was happy that I was coming to Him with something that I desired.

I went dress shopping a couple times with my sisters, but nothing really jumped out at me. I wasn't even sure what I was looking for. I needed to use my agency to try to get a better idea of what I really wanted. I prayed and asked God to help me see what was really in my heart regarding the dress I desired. That night I had a dream. In the dream, I saw myself wearing a gorgeous red dress. It had straight lines, was form fitting, and had a high neck and collar. There was lace throughout the pattern and it looked stunning. I loved that the dress was lacy because it fit my name! When I woke up, I still had that image in my mind and an instant love for the dress. I knew it was the dress I wanted.

That day, one of my sisters called and offered to watch my children so I could go dress shopping again that evening. Another sister called and asked if I wanted to go dress shopping with her again. We went to a couple

stores, but didn't find anything. Finally, we were walking out of a store in the mall that had many beautiful dresses, but none like the red dress I had seen in my dream. We were almost to the exit when I saw a discount rack off in the corner. I walked over to the rack and started to look through the dresses on it. Almost immediately, I saw this beautiful red dress. It had a lace overlay and the high collar, just like I had seen in my dream. I knew it was my dress. The size and price were not marked on the dress, but it fit me perfectly when I tried it on. I came out to show my sister and knew from her reaction that it was a stunning dress. I had to get it. When I got to the check-out, I was surprised at the price as well. It really was on clearance and was cheaper than what I had budgeted for.

As soon as I got out of the store, I shouted "God is amazing!" I told my sister about my dream and that this dress resembled the dress I had dreamed of so closely. I was so happy and amazed. When I went to the banquet, I felt like I was wearing a miracle. I was excited about my perfect dress, and even more excited about how God brought it into my life.

Lacey's experience with the red dress illustrates how she really embraced her personal power by using her agency to choose what she wanted. She decided that she wanted a fancy new dress. She did not give her agency away by letting fear of what others would think tell her that her desire was frivolous or materialistic. She prayed that God would help her to understand what she really

desired so that she could get even more excited about it. She used her agency to decide what she wanted and then allowed God to bring it to her. When you use the principles in this book to partner with God, you will have experiences similar to this one. It all starts by owning your agency and being willing to choose what you desire.

Agency is crucial to the creation process. First, agency activates spiritual creation. When you choose to desire something, you start to create it spiritually. We will discuss this more in chapter 8 when we talk about hope. Agency is also essential to creation because you have to use your agency over and over again to stay connected to God's power throughout the creation process. The next section in this book tells you how to do that through achieving and maintaining balance with God. Chapters 2–6 discuss what balance is, how to know when you are out of balance, and tools that you can use to stay balanced throughout the day. Staying balanced is a critical part of the creation process.

# Part 1: Balance

# Chapter 2
## Being in Balance with God

One of the most important ways you will use your agency in the creation process is choosing to be connected to God. We call this being in balance. Balance is another fundamental concept in this book because achieving a daily state of balance with God brings peace and enables you to effectively partner with God in the creation process. We define balance as follows:

*Balance = a state of peace and contentment that results from being connected to and partnered with God*

When you are balanced, you are able to receive power and direction from God. You feel good about your life, are present in the moment, and feel content. Balance also enables the creation process to flow smoothly.

### The Balance Scale

Being balanced with God might not look the way you think it looks. Balance does not mean that you and God

are both working as hard as you can to make something happen. Balance is about you pulling back enough to let God operate fully in your life.

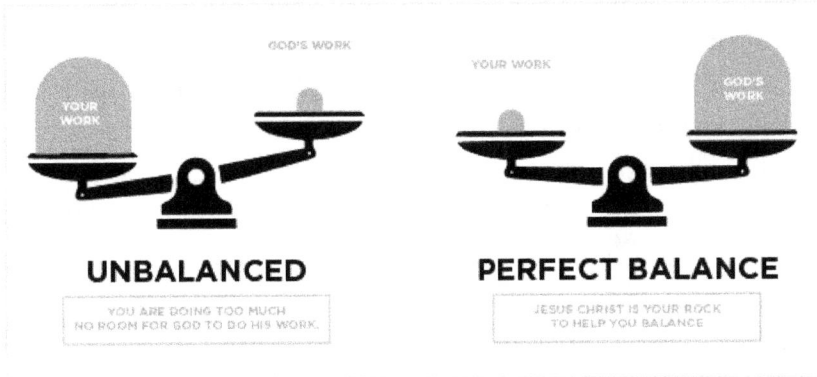

GOD'S WORK
YOUR WORK
YOUR WORK
GOD'S WORK

**UNBALANCED**  **PERFECT BALANCE**

YOU ARE DOING TOO MUCH
NO ROOM FOR GOD TO DO HIS WORK.

JESUS CHRIST IS YOUR ROCK
TO HELP YOU BALANCE

**Figure 1: The Balance Scale**

Figure 1 illustrates this. It shows a scale that you are trying to balance over an apex. Your work is represented by a weight on the left of the scale. This is everything that God expects you to contribute to solving your problems and creating your desires. This area encompasses all the things you can engage in that will help you to meet God in partnership in your life. The weight on the right is God's work. This weight represents what God is doing—and can do—for you. It represents everything that God desires to contribute to your life. The major point of this illustration is to show that you and God can be co-producing your life together; you both have contributions to make to your success. Perfect balance is when your contributions are exactly what they need to be and God can show up and do most of the work (see second panel). Instead of you trying to do as much as possible and only leaving a little room

for God to contribute, you scale back your efforts and give God more room to operate in your life.

The primary way to get out of balance is to try to do too much and not leave enough space in your life for God's work. This approach is represented by the saying "God helps those who help themselves." You might use this mantra to reinforce the belief that you have to put forth immense personal effort before you can be worthy of or merit any help from God. However, when you feel that receiving what you want in life is primarily (or even solely) dependent upon your efforts, then you are not leaving enough space for God. You are not trusting God to do His part.

The truth is that God desires to help you, bless you, and contribute to your life. God is an expert at applying wisdom, energy, and power to solve your problems. When you start doing too much, you are taking a portion of God's work upon yourself. God honors that because He honors your agency, even if your choice reduces the amount of work that He can do for you. You may think that doing more and controlling more will speed up the process of getting what you desire, but it will not. It actually slows the whole process down because you have reduced God's contributions. If you believe that you have to do it all on your own, then you might try to push God out entirely. In those instances, you rapidly burn yourself out and end up pushing yourself further and further out of balance as you become frustrated, angry, overwhelmed, or disappointed.

We illustrate this with an example. Marjorie and Janice have each written a novel, and they want to get their novels published. Marjorie has heard that there are obstacles to publishing for the first time. Either she has to have

a lot of money upfront to self-publish the book, or she has to work really hard to find a publisher who is willing to publish her book. But she isn't daunted by this challenge. She researches publishing companies and reaches out to each company to ask them to publish her novel. She talks to book agents to see if they can help her get published. She writes letters and sends emails and spends hours and hours on the phone. After six months, she is feeling very frustrated and angry at all of the rejections that she has gotten. She keeps praying for God's help, but she doesn't feel like He is really helping her. The process has been so much harder than she anticipated. But she really wants to publish this book; she must publish it! She redoubles her efforts and starts sending more emails, writing more letters, and making more phone calls. She attends workshops and listens to podcasts. She even prays more. She is exhausted. Finally, after a year of putting in non-stop time and effort, Marjorie finds a publisher who is willing to publish her book. Although she knew that God was helping her, the process felt long and difficult.

Janice, on the other hand, takes a different approach. She knows that she could easily get overwhelmed by all of the things that people tell her she needs to do in order to get published. But she has had experience turning her life and her goals over to God, so she knows that God does not expect her to wear herself out trying to get published. Instead, she focuses on being in balance with God and trying to do what she feels inspired to do. One day she wakes up and feels inspired to read some blogs about publishing. A week later she feels inspired to write a cover letter and send it to a few publishers. The next week she has the idea to think about what she wants for cover art.

A month after deciding to get published, Janice is about to board a flight across the country to visit her parents. At the last minute, she feels like she wants to take a copy of her manuscript to proofread and edit on the plane. As she is marking up her manuscript, the person sitting next to her asks her what she is doing. They start a conversation, and she finds out that the person sitting next to her is a book agent. The agent asks to read the first chapter of her novel and based on what she reads, she asks Janice to send her the full novel. Janice emails her novel as soon as she arrives at her destination. Later that week, Janice gets a call from the agent. The agent loves her book and feels that she knows a publisher or two who would be interested in it. Within a few weeks, the agent has negotiated publication with one of the publishers.

What is the difference in these two stories? Marjorie worked as if the whole project depended on her—because she felt that it did. She did not trust that things would work out if she did not do all of the leg work. She essentially minimized God's contributions because she was afraid that if she was not working on publishing all of the time that it wouldn't happen. She achieved her goal, but only after expending maximum amounts of time and effort. Janice, on the other hand, was more in balance with God. She knew that there were steps that she would have to take, but she trusted God to show her those steps as she needed to take them. She was okay going for days or even weeks without specific direction because she trusted that God was working on this. In the end, her journey to publication was much smoother, easier, and faster because she remained in balance with God the whole time. She did not fall into patterns of fear and frustration. She trusted God

to do His part, and she trusted that she had done enough. Janice focused on staying in balance with God rather than on publishing her book. Marjorie was focused on publishing her book, but did not realize that her overexertion had pulled her out of balance with God and limited what He could do for her. That was why she felt that God was not answering her prayers. She was not giving Him room to do so! She was trying to micromanage and control the whole process herself.

It is important to believe that God wants to work on your behalf. God wants to give you 100 percent of what He can do, but you might not be letting Him. You might want to control the whole process because you are afraid that if you don't, you will not receive what you desire. You may feel that you have to put forth a certain amount of effort in order to be worthy of God's help. Your fear makes you take too much upon yourself and push God out of the process—even while you are simultaneously asking for God's help. When you try to do God's work, you are limiting His power and energy in your life. Ironically, by doing more, you actually accomplish less and slow down your progress toward receiving what you desire because you have limited what God can do for you—just like Marjorie did in the example above.

Unfortunately, you've probably been taught that hard work is the path to getting what you want. If you are religious, then you might add to that the belief that you have to do a certain amount before God will bless you—that you have to earn God's help or blessings. You might resist the idea that you can do less and leave more to God. Yet it is a true principle. The idea that you must earn God's help

**49**

or put forth a lot of effort to show that you are worthy of His blessings is false.

You are enough exactly as you are. God loves you completely and unconditionally. God *never* withholds power and help from you. God is willing to provide you with His full power exactly as you are right now. God helps you all the time simply because He loves you and because you ask for it. You do not have to earn His help or meet some standard of worthiness to receive His help. Instead of the old mantra of "God helps those who help themselves," we invite you to adopt a new, truer, more powerful mantra: "God helps those who believe that He helps them." You show that belief by staying in balance; a balanced person is in a state of believing in God's help and deliverance. We repeat: *The only thing you have to do to receive God's help is to be in balance with Him and ask for His help.* You only have to do what God inspires you to do and then leave the rest to God.

We cannot emphasize enough that you are probably doing too much to meet your goals or receive your desires. You might be spending more time pushing out God rather than receiving what He is offering you. Most people spend more time being out of balance than being in balance. If you are truly seeking a more joyful, peaceful life, then you need to stop trying to force your goals to happen and focus more of your time and energy on staying in balance. Retreating from your efforts to receive what you desire may feel counterintuitive. However, if you listen closely, your heart will tell you that there is a better way than just pushing yourself too hard and beating yourself up too much. The better way starts by getting into balance and staying there.

## Recognizing When You Are in Balance

Your emotions, thoughts, and physical state all provide clues that can help you recognize whether you are in balance with God or not.

### Emotional Balance

When you are balanced, you feel joyful, peaceful, happy, and more positive in general. You feel open to giving and receiving love. Balance is a peaceful, happy state. When you are balanced, you might feel an impulse to sing or dance. You might find yourself laughing often. You just feel content, even when you are doing tasks that you do not usually enjoy. Balance makes every aspect of your life feel good. When you are balanced, you are present in the moment and enjoying whatever is right in front of you.

Balance means that you are at peace with feeling the full range of your emotions. While balance is characterized by emotions that make you feel lighter and happier, it does not mean that you do not ever feel sadness, anger, or fear. Instead, it means that those emotions flow through you and dissipate rather than remaining and overwhelming you. The natural, balanced emotional state is allowing your emotions to flow naturally rather than resisting or avoiding them. Emotions are not meant to linger. When you acknowledge your emotions and give yourself permission to feel them, they shift into a new emotion. Balance gives you a greater perspective on your emotions, so the ebb and flow of your emotions does not bother you. You notice your emotions without reacting to them. You trust that when you choose to feel each emotion, it will soon pass and reveal the next emotion. When you are balanced, there is a pervading feeling of calm and peace, even if anger or fear temporarily surfaces. You feel a sense

**51**

of peace when you allow yourself to feel anger or fear, because you know those feelings will soon shift into a greater sense of peace. Feeling an undesired emotion does not mean you are out of balance. Resisting and avoiding your emotions is what can pull you out of balance.

When you are not balanced, you tend to feel overwhelmed, anxious, stressed, frustrated, or apathetic. You dwell on those emotions and hold on to them. When you are out of balance, those emotions get stuck, and you might feel them most of the time. You might even react to them and feel angry or afraid of the emotions you are feeling. The fear, overwhelm, anger, or sorrow can lead you into judging and blaming yourself and others—actions that pull you further out of balance. You might dislike these emotions so much that you try to avoid feeling them. You might keep yourself busy with work or household tasks, or you might waste time engaging in some mindless activity, like watching TV or scrolling through social media feeds on your phone. Additionally, when you are not balanced, you might feel shut down in your heart, feeling unloved and unloving. Consequently, you might feel like withdrawing from other people or shutting them out physically or emotionally. Emotional turmoil is a sign of imbalance.

### Mental Balance

When you are in balance, you receive and process information in an organized, balanced, and efficient manner. Your thoughts are clear and flow peacefully from one thought to the next. In a balanced state, you are not fighting with your mind for control; you can quiet your thoughts when you need to. It is easy for you to focus on your tasks rather than being caught up in the regrets of the past or worries about the future. In a balanced state,

you naturally make decisions that make you feel confident. You make decisions much faster because your choice often just feels right. Because your mind is calm and still, it is easier for you to receive God's guidance and direction for you. Your thoughts tend to be more positive, uplifting, and supportive of your goals and the life you desire. When you are in balance, your mind serves you well and makes your life easier.

An unbalanced mind is experienced as constant stress. When you are out of balance, your thoughts are scattered and you struggle to stay focused. Your mind might seem like it is racing out of control. You might become overwhelmed by all of the input from your senses and feel paralyzed about making decisions. When you do make a decision, you second-guess yourself. When you are out of balance your thoughts will be more negative, defeating, and limiting. You will often have critical thoughts directed toward yourself and others. When you are not in balance, you will not be present with what you are doing in the moment. Instead, you will be thinking about experiences in the past or worrying about future outcomes. Imbalance is represented by being trapped in cycle of worry, doubt, and concern.

### *Physical Balance*

Your physical body can also help you to recognize when you are in balance with God. When you are balanced, your bodily functions happen naturally, smoothly, and effectively. You feel good. You have more energy and stamina. You feel more rested and get better sleep. Your body feels strong and generally in good health. When you are in balance, you also feel a desire to take care of your physical body through eating healthful foods, getting

sufficient sleep, and engaging in exercise. You feel more at peace with your body.

When you are not balanced, you feel the opposite—dreariness, pain, sickness, or disease. You might feel excessively fatigued. Additionally, a prolonged imbalance can lead to chronic conditions and illnesses, such as chronic pain. When you are not in balance, you do not feel like taking care of your body and are not mindful of the choices that you make regarding diet, exercise, and sleep. You feel that you are at war with your body or that your body is your enemy.

Your emotions, thoughts, and sensations in your body can help you to see whether you are in balance or not. You feel content, peaceful, and confident when you are in balance, and life is dreary and overwhelming when you are not. As you focus on staying mindful and focused on the present moment, you will be more in tune with the signals your body is sending you about whether you are in balance. Your emotional, mental, and physical states all provide important information to you about how balanced you are with God. Practice watching for and listening to those signals. When you notice that you are out of balance, you can get back into balance using the concepts we discuss in chapters 4–6. For now, practice noticing how balanced you are throughout the day.

# Chapter 3
## Balance Gives You Access to God's Power

Balance is crucial to creation because it gives you full access to God's power. Figure 2 illustrates this point. Consider a timeline. Your timeline stretches to the past on the left and the future on the right. The center of the line is the present moment, right now. Now imagine that your present moment is enclosed in a circle. The circle represents God's timeline. God actually operates outside of the construct of Earth time, which is why we depict His timeline as a circle. All time—the past, present, and future—is before God at any moment.[4] The middle of God's circular timeline is the present. God's experience of the present is encircled by His knowledge of the past and future. Your present and God's complete timeline coincide in the present moment.

---

[4] "But they reside in the presence of God, on a globe like a sea of glass and fire, where all things for their glory are manifest, past, present, and future, and are continually before the Lord." Doctrine and Covenants 130:7

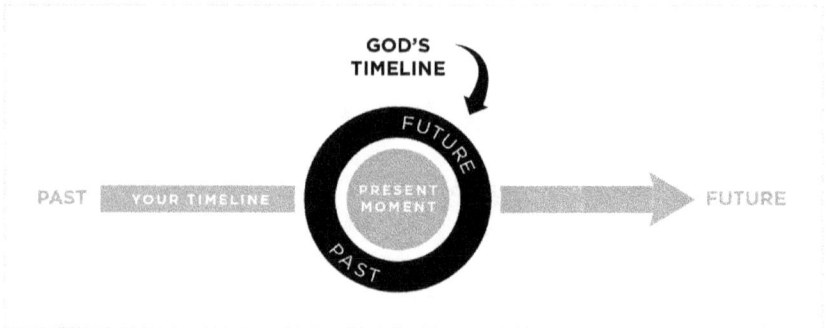

**Figure 2: Intersection of Your Timeline and God's Timeline**

The present moment is when you have access to the most power from God. It is the moment where God can show up for you completely—if you choose to allow Him. You do so by choosing to be in balance with God in the present moment. You are not thinking about regrets and pain from the past, and you are not worrying about how things will work out in the future. You are just completely focused on being present in that moment and being connected to God. This gives you full access to all of God's power, including the power to create and the power to experience the life you desire. Staying fully aware helps you to know when you are out of balance so you can reconnect with God and re-access His power.

Thus, a necessary condition for being in balance is being mindful in the present moment. Many authors and teachers have discussed the importance of mindfulness, so this is likely not a new concept for you. We share the Merriam-Webster definition of mindfulness.

*Mindfulness = "the practice of maintaining a nonjudgmental state of heightened or complete*

*awareness of one's thoughts, emotions, or experi-*
*ences on a moment-to-moment basis"*[5]

Mindfulness is a state of awareness, and it can only happen in the present moment. It is being aware of what you are doing and the input you are getting from your five senses. It is also an awareness of what is going on inside of you— emotions, thoughts, and sensations of your body. Mindfulness is powerful because it grounds you fully in the present moment—the place where you can fully access God's power. You have to forsake thoughts of the past and the future in order to be completely mindful. Mindfulness is a tool that helps you stay in balance because it enables you to recognize if you are balanced or not.

There is a beautiful passage in the New Testament about mindfulness. In the Sermon on the Mount, Jesus taught:

*"And why take ye thought for raiment? Consider*
*the lilies of the field, how they grow; they toil not,*
*neither do they spin: And yet I say until you, That*
*even Solomon in all his glory was not arrayed like*
*one of these"* (Matthew 6:28–29).

This passage illustrates God's willingness, desire, and ability to bless His children. If God can take care of lilies and sparrows and all life on Earth, then He can certainly care for you. God supplies everything that the plants and animals need to grow. He is willing to supply all of that to you. God can heal your past and provide for your future. You allow God to do so when you stay grounded and

---

[5] https://www.merriam-webster.com/dictionary/mindfulness

balanced in the present moment. By using your agency to choose balance, you activate God's help in your life. Then God can give you everything you need in each moment. God deeply desires to bless you with this.

Jesus continued:

*"Wherefore, if God so clothe the grass of the field, which to day is, and to morrow is cast into the oven, shall he not much more clothe you, O ye of little faith? Therefore, take no thought, saying, What shall we eat? or, What shall we drink? or, Wherewithal shall we be clothed? . . . [For] your Heavenly Father knoweth that ye have need of all these things"* (Matthew 6:30–32).

Seek the kingdom of God first and then all the things you are seeking—food, clothing, shelter—will be given to you. You might interpret "seeking the kingdom of God" as serving and working to literally build God's kingdom through church service. We suggest an alternative interpretation. What if seeking the kingdom of God meant pausing in each moment and checking your balance with God? Perhaps seeking to be in balance with God is seeking His kingdom and making that kingdom part of yourself. By staying in balance and connected to God, you allow Him to bring all things to you. When you are in the kingdom of God, you feel peace, confidence, and trust—exactly how you will feel when you are balanced in the present moment. Perhaps the kingdom of God is not a place you go to, but a state of being you can achieve right now. This scripture illustrates God's great willingness to bless you with abundance—everything in His kingdom.

Jesus concluded this passage by saying:

*"But seek ye first the kingdom of God, and his righteousness; and all these things shall be added unto you. Take therefore no thought for the morrow: for the morrow shall take thought for the things of itself." (Matthew 6:33–34)*

You are counseled to take no thought for tomorrow. That is mindfulness—being aware, grounded, and connected to God in the present moment. Jesus is telling you to stop worrying about the future and to stay focused on feeling peace in the moment. You may struggle to stay mindful and present in the moment because you are worrying about the future. This could include thinking about other things on your to-do list or trying to make a plan to accomplish your goals. It could include worrying about the consequences of one of your decisions—or a loved one's decisions. It might also take the form of dreading situations that you think will be unpleasant, difficult, boring, or painful. Worry is future focused. It is fear that the future might bring discomfort or pain. You may spend a lot of time worrying about things in the future and formulating plans to avoid pain and difficulties rather than focusing on what is happening in the present.

Thoughts of the past also prevent mindfulness and balance in the moment and can have the same negative effect on you. You might dwell on something you did or said that caused you to feel guilt, pain, or shame. You might dwell on mistakes from the past or things that others have done to wrong or hurt you. You can get addicted to thinking about past traumatic events and replaying them

in your mind. Thoughts of the past can also pull you out of the present moment.

Jesus taught that when you are balanced and aware in the present moment, your past and future are taken care of. If there is something in your past that needs to be healed, God will bring it up at the right moment for healing. If there is a plan you need to make for the future, God will reveal it to you. In those moments when you step out of balance and focus on either the past or the future, you are striking out on your own rather than allowing God to do His work. Stay balanced in the present moment, and you will have the power that you need to create the abundant life that you desire. Your life will flow peacefully. You will be in a state of peace and joy and love. Miracles will become a regular occurrence in your life.

## Becky's Story About Living out of Balance

In my story in the introduction, I shared with you that a big turning point in my life was that day that I realized that my hair was falling out because I was under so much stress. I was trying too hard to do it all—be successful at work, keep an organized and tidy house, have good relationships, and do all of the church service that I could possibly do. Not only would I do all of these things, but I would try to put my best effort into everything and make it as perfect as I possibly could. I was unsatisfied if I did less than my best work. It was an exhausting and difficult way to live!

The worst part was living in constant fear, worry, doubt, and concern about how things were going to turn out and whether I would be able to deliver on all of my promises. I was constantly worried about having enough time to do

all of the tasks on my list. Even when I was in the middle of a task, my mind would wander to thinking about the future, such as planning what I would do next. I struggled to be present and enjoy the things I was doing. I remember being excited to start taking dance lessons because it was something I had always wanted to do. However, my life felt so busy and I was so worried about getting everything done that the dance class became more of a burden than a fun activity. It was hard for me to enjoy dancing when I was so worried about how I would get everything done. I struggled to keep my mind focused on what I was doing because I was always afraid about meeting all of my external and self-imposed deadlines.

Living with constant fear for years took a major toll on my body. I now understand that because I spent years ignoring the mental and emotional signals that I was out of balance, my physical body started to try to get my attention. Its complaints grew louder and louder until I could not ignore them any longer. Not only was my hair falling out, but I was gaining weight, feeling tired all the time, grinding my teeth, having major insomnia, and experiencing tight muscles in my neck, shoulders, and back. I was pretty miserable. It was only when I became so alarmed at all of these physical symptoms of stress—fear that I had stuffed down for years—that I was willing to try to find another way to live my life.

I have learned a lot by reflecting on how my life got to that crisis point. I realized that during those years, I spent most of my time trying to please others. I was doing the things that I thought other people—and even God—expected of me or wanted me to do. I was giving my agency away. I was letting my fear of what other people

would think of me—or my desire for others to see me as a certain kind of person—dictate how I spent my time rather than taking care of myself or choosing those activities that would serve my greatest and highest good. For example, I had a really hard time saying "no" if someone at church asked me to help with something. Even if my schedule was already full and I was already feeling stressed, I would agree to help whenever I was asked. I wasn't really making choices for my life; I was just giving my agency away and letting others determine how I used my time.

I realized that my stress and fear were all due to the fact that I was doing too much. I was trying to do everything myself and there was very little room for God to work in my life, despite my constant pleadings for help. I would pray and I felt blessed many, many times. But I see now that I was unwilling to let go of control. I was not sure if God would really pull through for me, so I was reluctant to turn my life over to Him. I was unwilling to step back enough to let God's full power into my life. I spent years thinking that if I just worked harder and longer and smarter, that I could outrun the stress. I now understand that is not possible. I firmly believe that the only way for me to have peace amid the chaos of life is to seek to be balanced with God every day. My to-do lists are still long, even as I am getting better at claiming my agency and saying "no" to things that do not serve me. I cannot achieve peace by getting everything done on my lists—because it will never get completely done. For me, peace only comes when I take the steps necessary to get balanced with God again. Then I can work through my lists and accomplish my tasks with focus and peace.

This is a blessing to me now. It is very easy for me to see the emotional, mental and physical signs that I am feeling stress. I know that stress and overwhelm mean that I am out of balance with God and that the most important thing I can do is to get back into balance, even if it means not doing something perfectly or being late on a deadline. Anytime I use the word stressful to describe my day, I know that I need to reset and get back into balance. I am not perfect at this yet, but I spend a lot more time in balance with God than I used to. I feel so much more peace and joy than I ever have, and I feel excited for the future rather than dread. I love knowing that I have a proven method to help me find peace when life gets stressful.

Maintaining your balance with God throughout the day is crucial for creating your heart's desires. Balance means that you are allowing God's full power into your life instead of blocking it out by trying to do too much. You are also standing in your full power because you used your agency to choose balance instead of imbalance. Together you and God are an unstoppable team when you are balanced and connected. When you discover that you are not in balance, then you can make the choice to get back into balance with God. That is the topic of the next chapter.

# Chapter 4
## Choosing Balance

Maintaining a balanced state with God will help you to create a life you love. The creation tools in this book only work when you prioritize your balance with God. This requires the active use of your agency because you must choose to be in balance with God moment after moment. God will respond to you immediately whenever you seek balance because God also desires that you are balanced and connected to Him. The process of getting back into balance is straightforward and easy. Sometimes the hardest part of the process is trusting that it really is easy.

### Getting Back Into Balance

There are four simple steps to get yourself back into balance: recognize, choose, pray, and allow. First, you must recognize that you are not in balance. Be mindful of your emotional, mental, and physical state so that you can identify those moments when you are out of balance. As we discussed in the prior chapter, your emotions, thoughts, and physical sensations are all important signals

about the strength of your connection to God in any given moment. If life starts getting bumpy and you suspect that you are out of balance, then stop for a moment and take a few deep breaths. Pay attention to what you feel—emotionally, mentally, and physically. Are you feeling grumpy, sad, or frustrated? Is your mind spinning and unfocused? Is your body more tired and run down than usual? If you answer "yes" to any of those questions, then you are out of balance. Recognize that you are and choose to accept it. You have the right to feel the way you do, and it is nothing to be ashamed of. Take responsibility for the fact that you are out of balance, but try to do so from a state of neutral acceptance rather than being angry at yourself. That anger will pull you further out of balance. Your goal is to simply recognize when you are out of balance and to accept it.

The second step is choosing to be in balance. When you recognize that you are out of balance, then ask yourself: do you want to keep feeling this way? In order to have balance, you must be willing to let go of how you are currently feeling. For example, imagine that someone in your family said something that made you really angry, and you have been dwelling on that anger all day. In the evening, as you reflect on your bad day, you realize that you are out of balance because you are stuck in anger. Now you have a choice: do you want to keep holding on to that anger or do you desire to be in balance? If you choose balance, then activate your agency toward balance. You can even say: *I choose to get back into balance with God.*

The third step is to pray to God and ask to be restored to balance. Tell God your desire to be in balance with Him. It does not need to be a long or involved prayer. You are simply telling God your desire to be in balance and asking

for God's help getting back into balance. Let God know of your desire to be in balance. A simple prayer could be: *God, I have stepped out of balance again. I recognize it, and I don't want to stay here. I choose to be back with you. I want to be back with you. Please restore me back to balance. Thank you.* Balance is not something that you can achieve on your own; God restores you to balance. You must ask God for balance in order to receive it. Your awareness and agency are required in this process because God will not impose balance on you if you do not desire it. If you choose to keep feeling angry, God will accept your choice. However, if you desire balance, God will bless you with that. You get to choose what you want, but, ultimately, being restored to balance is a gift to you from God.

Finally, allow yourself to be restored to balance. Sit back. Breathe. Feel yourself getting back into balance. Feel God's presence and power helping you to do so. Avoid questioning or wondering whether it is happening. Just trust that it is and choose to accept the gift that God is offering you. God *always* responds when you ask for balance. There are no requirements other than asking. Trust that the gift is there for you. Feel and express gratitude for the balance as it comes. Allow yourself to move on to your next task or activity and trust that balance will come.

That is all that it takes. It is as easy as that. A choice and a quick prayer are the perfect way to reset, especially after you have been practicing balance for a while. Often, the hardest part is believing that a simple prayer is enough to restore you to balance. Keep engaging in the process and trust that it is working. You will begin to see evidence that God is honoring your choice and blessing you with balance. At first, you might need to go through these steps

many times throughout the day in order to stay in balance. The important thing is to stay aware and keep noticing when you are out of balance. Then take a moment to stop, breathe, notice how you feel, and get back into balance. Do it over and over again. The more you do this, the easier it will be for you to stay in balance and the longer you will be able to maintain balance. Remember that you are not doing this on your own. God is assisting you and providing you with the balance you desire.

Although we presented four steps to get into balance, there really is no one right way to get back into balance. We simply list these steps as a starting point for people who are new to this process. Do what works for you. As you practice and experiment, you might find techniques for getting into balance that work better for you. We trust that recognizing you are out of balance, activating your agency, praying, and allowing the balance to come will benefit you in your quest for greater balance.

## Visualization for Getting Into Balance

It can be challenging to get back into balance when you are not used to this process. There might also be times when you feel trapped in a strong emotion, such as fear, overwhelm, sorrow, or pain. In those instances, the following visualization exercise can help you to get into balance. We also recommend this longer visualization when you are still learning to trust that a simple prayer can restore you to balance.

Before beginning this visualization, go to a quiet place where you will not be disturbed. Get into a comfortable position. It is typically better to do this in a sitting position rather than lying down so that you do not fall asleep. Close your eyes. Now take a slow, deep breath in through

your nose and then slowly exhale through your mouth. Take another breath—an even deeper breath. And exhale. Then take a third, deep breath. Again, exhale. Try to remember to continue taking deep, slow breaths throughout the visualization.

Relax your body and mind. Picture a tranquil, quiet place. You do not need to direct or control your thoughts. If dark or unpleasant thoughts enter your mind, accept them and avoid judgment. Allow whatever comes into your mind. Merely picture a quiet place in your mind.

When you can see the place in your mind, picture yourself walking into that quiet scene, as if you are watching a movie of yourself on a big screen in your mind. Allow yourself to feel whatever emotions are keeping you from being in balance—anger, fear, sadness, or any other emotion. Visualize yourself reacting to that emotion. You might see yourself sitting down and crying. You might be crouching in fear or overwhelm. You might be waving your fist in anger or frustration. Again, allow whatever comes. Trust your intuition and trust what shows up for you. The important thing is to fully feel whatever emotion has caused you to get out of balance and to try to create a vivid picture of it in your mind. Stay with that image as long as you desire.

Now imagine that you see yourself raise your head up toward heaven and toward God. Remember that God loves you perfectly, and He always responds when you call out to Him. Now see and hear yourself calling out to God from that place: *God, I feel so angry and hurt and overwhelmed. I*

*desire to be with you. I desire to surrender these emotions to you. I desire to be back in balance with you. Please help me.*

Visualize yourself looking up at the sky. Now imagine a thick golden rope descending toward you from heaven. Watch the rope as it descends until it is right in front of you. When the rope has fully descended, imagine yourself taking hold of it and securing yourself with it. You might tie it around your waist or just hold it. See yourself connected securely to that rope.

Then take another deep breath. Keep seeing yourself looking up toward God and holding tightly to the rope. Then pray: *God, please receive me. I choose to be with you. I ask you to receive me where you are.* See yourself being pulled up toward heaven by this beautiful, golden rope. Feel the movement of rising steadily upward. Feel your emotions shift as you move upward. The rope is pulling you up to a healthier, happier, holier place. You are going up to heaven! Relax and enjoy the movement. You can even imagine yourself throwing out your arms as if you are flying through the air. Feel yourself elevating.

Watch as this rope pulls you up through a cloud or a veil that separates a new, higher environment from the place where you started. The colors here are more beautiful, light, and vibrant. It is a world of pure white light. Everywhere you look, there is a warm, friendly, welcoming light. Now that you are safely in this new place, you can let go of the rope.

Visualize yourself looking around this new, light-filled place. If you see any remnants of the original picture, like darker colors or unpleasant objects, then see yourself putting your hands on those colors or objects. Keep repeating in your mind the phrase: *I love you. I love you. I*

*love you.* Do this until the dark colors or unpleasant objects are replaced by light and vibrant colors. When all vestiges of the original scene are gone, relax, take a deep breath, and see this bright, beautiful new world.

There might be a person or people in this new world— your heavenly parents, Jesus Christ, an angel, or a deceased loved one. You might not see anyone at all. Allow yourself to look around and enjoy what is there. This is a place of peace, love and protection. This is the place where God resides. It is a place of perfect balance and love. Take a deep breath and feel the wonderful light energy of this place. Allow it to enter into your heart and fill your whole being.

See yourself putting your hands on your heart and praying: *Thank you, God. I am in balance now. Thank you for helping me to get to this place of balance. I choose to remain here with you. Thank you for helping me and sharing this beautiful place with me.*

You can stay in this meditative space as long as you want. Enjoy how good it feels. Feel the peace that enters your heart. This is a wonderful, miraculous space. Anything you desire for your life can be created from this space. Miracles originate from this space. Stay there and enjoy it as long as you desire. Continue to breathe deeply. Choose to be with God. Choose to be in this space of pure light and love. Praise and thank God for bringing you into this wonderful space.

When you are ready, allow your awareness to return to your body and the room that you are in. Take another deep, slow breath. You are done. Tune in to how you feel. Do you feel balanced? Do you feel stillness in your mind and heart? Do you feel ready to walk into the next moment,

fully partnered with God? If not, do the visualization a second time. When you feel restored to balance, then go about your regular activities and strive to be fully present as you do each one.

This visualization is a great way to get yourself back into balance. Do this first thing in the morning to start your day with God. Do it before you go to bed so you can fall asleep while in this beautiful, peaceful space. Do this at any point throughout the day when you feel you have been yanked out of balance by the events of the day and your reaction to them. If you forget to do this, do not judge yourself or be hard on yourself; this will only pull you further out of balance. Instead of chastising yourself, do the visualization in that moment to help yourself get unstuck. Do this visualization as often as needed to help you maintain your balance.

As you keep doing this visualization, it will get easier and start to feel more natural. The exact visualization is not important. For example, it also works if you visualize a hot air balloon or giant eagle taking you up into the light realm. The important elements of the visualization are beginning with the awareness that you are feeling trapped in an unpleasant space, praying for God's help, seeing Him send you a way to get up to where He is, and allowing yourself to arrive in that new light realm where God dwells. You are not limited to experiencing this visualization in any particular way. Make the visualization work for you. The visualization will be more powerful for you if it is personal, rather than trying to imagine the same

visual as another person. Once you get to the light realm and feel peaceful and content, try to hold on to those feelings throughout your day. If you lose them, repeat the visualization.

## Trust That God Will Show Up for You

For most people, getting into balance is not the hardest part of this process. The biggest challenge is staying aware of whether you are in balance. It is easy to recognize when you are in balance, but you are probably very good at powering through the physical, mental, and emotional signals that indicate a lack of balance. In your haste to get things done or to meet the needs of those around you, you push aside the emotions and spinning thoughts that indicate that you are out of balance. It takes a great deal of attention and mindfulness to monitor your balance, and you are probably not used to focusing your attention on balance when there are so many other things and people demanding your attention.

You are fighting against years and years of society's messages that have taught you that you need to do more and be more productive. You might be living an over-programmed life where your time and attention are constantly being sucked into many different commitments. You might not have learned how to just *be* with God in a moment of stillness. At first, you will probably spend a lot of time worrying about things in the future or feeling regret about the past. It will take some time and practice to let some of those things go in order to stay balanced.

The best way to stay in balance is to focus on what you are doing in the present moment, whether that's working, doing the dishes, reading to your child, or driving in your car. When you mind wanders to other things, bring it

back to focus on what you are doing right in the moment. Perhaps you are cooking dinner for your family. While you are cooking, your mind keeps wandering to a big presentation that you are doing at work the next day. You feel that you have more preparation to do for that meeting, and you are fearful that you will not have enough time to get it done. You start thinking of all of the other things that you need to do tonight—replacing a lightbulb, putting away some laundry, helping a child with a school project, feeding the dog, getting the kids to bed, returning a phone call from your brother, making a grocery list, and spending a few minutes of quality time with your spouse. As you keep thinking about the other things you need to do, you get more worried and stressed. You are afraid that you will not be able to do all of these things. These thoughts have pulled you out of balance. You are no longer living in the present moment. Instead, you are trying to live in the future—planning what you need to do and worrying about your presentation.

When you recognize that you are out of balance, you can say a quick prayer and ask God to get you back into balance. You can even shut your eyes for a moment and do a quick visualization to help you get balanced. Then, to help you stay in balance, practice keeping your mind focused on the present moment and what you are doing. Use your five senses to help you. Returning to our making dinner example, notice how orange the carrot is. Feel the rough skin of that potato you are washing. Listen to the meat sizzling in the pan. Smell the aromas of the spices. If you are struggling to be present in the moment, stay focused on the input you get from your five senses. That will help to keep your mind focused on what you are doing

instead of wandering down a path that will pull you out of balance.

Another way to stay balanced and grounded in the present moment is to think about what you are grateful for, right in that moment. Be grateful for the food you have. Be grateful for the movement of your body that allows you to prepare it. Be grateful for the family that you will soon be feeding. Be grateful that preparing dinner gives you a break from work. Gratitude brings you back to the present moment and helps you to stay in balance.

It takes a lot of trust to believe that if you take the time and space to stay balanced that God will provide for all of your needs. One way to determine whether you are really trusting God is to see if you feel relief when you turn your burdens over to Him. As an example, suppose you are in charge of an important event. The morning of the event, you find out that the person who was supposed to order the catering dropped the ball and did not order the food. You are so stressed out! You still have to set up and decorate and take care of many other details before the event that night. There is no way that you can do all of that and take care of the food yourself. You call your friend in tears and ask for help. You can take care of everything else if your friend will figure out what to do for food for this event. Your friend says, "No problem. I know what to do. I'll take care of this and have the food there on time." As soon as your friend promises to do this, you feel immense relief. You know your friend is competent, and you trust her when she says that she can do this. You know that you can stop worrying about the food and focus on everything else. You feel such relief because your friend lifted that heavy burden off your shoulders.

Being in balance is like that feeling of relief. When you are balanced with God, you trust that He is taking care of the things you need Him to take care of for you. You can stop worrying about them because you know that your friend—God—is competent, and you can trust Him to pull through. That feeling of knowing that God has your back is part of being in balance with Him. The level of relief that you feel when you surrender something to God is a good measure of how much you trust God at that time. It is okay if your trust in God isn't perfect at this time—that is something that you can repent of and strengthen through repentance, which we will discuss in the next chapter.

The whole process requires a great deal of trust. It takes trust to believe that just saying a prayer or doing a visualization can help you get balanced again. It takes trust to believe that staying in balance is working for you. Your belief in the process will grow the more you keep trying. The more you experience moments of balance, the more uncomfortable you will be when you get out of balance. You will crave that feeling of being balanced again. Your trust in God will increase as you start to see Him show up more and more in your life.

## Self-Acceptance Facilitates Balance

It is easy for people to become hyper-focused on whether they are in balance after they learn about this concept. As you practice being balanced with God, you might start to worry about whether you are balanced enough, or you might get really down on yourself when you recognize that you have fallen out of balance. We encourage you to use balance as a tool to help you achieve peace rather than a bludgeon to beat yourself up with. If something in your

life has made you feel unworthy or feel that you are not enough, you might feel tempted to see yourself as a failure at getting into balance or staying in balance. This feeling will only pull you further out of balance.

You do not need to be perfectly in balance all of the time to receive God's help in your life. You do not need to be perfectly in balance all of the time to be a master creator. Perfection is not required. Do not create more anxiety in your life by constantly checking whether you are in balance or worrying about whether you are doing it right or being balanced enough. Just keep asking God to restore you to balance. Just keep trying to be present in the moment.

Self-acceptance is part of being in balance. When you are balanced with God, you feel more loving and accepting toward yourself. One way that you can practice getting into balance is by accepting that you are out of balance without criticizing or judging yourself. Choose to accept where you are in your journey toward greater balance. Choose to love yourself for trying and failing and trying again. The more grace and love you give to yourself, the easier it will be for you to maintain balance. This is a perfect opportunity to take more pressure off yourself and to put more trust in God.

There may be some really difficult challenges in your life that make it hard for you to stay in balance. You might have spent years living in worry and fear, and it can take some time to reprogram your mind and choose a new belief system that will allow you greater balance. The next chapter will help you with this. We'll discuss repentance and how to really work with Jesus Christ to change something in your life that you do not desire, particularly

stuck emotions or limiting beliefs. Whatever you lack in being balance with God can be healed and changed with Jesus Christ.

# Chapter 5
## Repentance

God will always restore you to balance when you ask. However, you may notice that you fall out of balance repeatedly due to the same issues. There might be some patterns in your life that you keep re-experiencing. For example, no matter how hard you try, you just cannot seem to stop snapping at your mother when she says innocuous, but annoying, things. You get angry and frustrated with yourself for doing it, but her words just seem to elicit an extreme emotional response from you. This pattern pulls you out of balance more often than you would like. The good news is that repentance brings in God's power to help you change unwanted patterns.

### What Is Repentance?

Repentance is turning away from anything in your life that separates you from God. The Bible Dictionary shares the following about repentance: "The Greek word of which this is the translation denotes a change of mind, a fresh view about God, about oneself, and about the world. Since we are born into conditions of mortality, repentance

comes to mean a turning of the heart and will to God..."[6] Repentance cleanses your mind and restores you to balance. It removes any mental or emotional patterns in your life that separate you from complete harmony and peace with God—from balance.

When you choose to repent, God transmutes you to a higher and holier state. According to Merriam-Webster, transmutation means "to change or alter in form, appearance, or nature and especially to a higher form."[7] Repentance allows God to elevate and change everything about you—your emotions, your thoughts, your actions, and your person. When you repent, God lifts you up and transforms you into a new person.

Temperature is a good analogy for transmutation. Everything on the planet has a temperature—a degree of warmth or coolness. If you have a carton of ice cream (something cold) and put it in the oven (someplace warm), then the ice cream will get warmer and melt. The warmer item raised the temperature of the colder item. If we apply this analogy to God, then God is the highest temperature on the scale—the hottest anything can be. Whenever you repent, you allow God's warmth to fill you and raise your temperature. If you repent over and over again, your temperature will continue to rise.

Anyone in a higher state (a hotter temperature in our analogy) can raise or elevate anything in a lower state (a lower temperature). This is how God elevates everyone and everything—because God is the highest of all. This is what people mean when they talk about God's grace. Merriam-Webster defines grace as "unmerited divine

[6] Bible Dictionary, Repentance; https://www.churchofjesuschrist.org/study/scriptures/bd/repentance?lang=eng
[7] https://www.merriam-webster.com/dictionary/transmuting

assistance given to humans for their regeneration or sanctification."[8] It is through God's grace that you are transmuted, or changed, into a better version of your-self. Repentance opens the door to God's grace and allows you to be elevated to a higher, better state. The more you repent, the more you become like God.

You have probably already experienced this in your life. You might have had an experience when you were angry about something. Perhaps you prayed to God and expressed all of that anger. You asked God to change your heart for you. After your prayer, you felt a feeling of peace or greater calm. You felt better because you invited and allowed God to change you. God gave you His grace and transmuted your emotions, beliefs, and energy into a higher state. This also happens when you pray and ask God to restore you to balance.

You might have also experienced this through your interactions with other people. Maybe you have had a pet die, and you felt really sad about it. Your friend came over and brought you flowers and talked to you. After your friend left, you felt better. Your friend was in a higher emotional state than you, so she had the power to lift you up and elevate your mood. You used your agency to allow her to lift you up.

By virtue of being your Savior and Redeemer, Jesus Christ has mastered grace. He is Deity, the most puri-fied and holy being in existence. Through His atonement, Christ has taken on a personal relationship with every-thing in existence, no matter what form it takes—matter, animals, plants, minerals, and humans. Christ com-pletely loves and accepts everything in existence. Anytime

[8] https://www.merriam-webster.com/dictionary/grace

anything comes into contact with Him, it is transmuted to a higher state through His grace. This transmutation takes place immediately upon contact; it is automatic. It happens every single time with no exceptions. Jesus Christ is continually transmuting everything around Him to elevate it closer to God's purified state. You just choose whether you desire to receive it or not.

A story from the New Testament illustrates this.

*"And a certain woman, which had an issue of blood twelve years, And she suffered many things of many physicians, and had spent all that she had, and was nothing bettered, but rather grew worse, When she had heard of Jesus, came in the press behind, and touched his garment.*

*For she said, If I may touch but his clothes, I shall be whole. And straightway the fountain of her blood was dried up; and she felt in her body that she was healed of that plague.*

*And Jesus, immediately knowing in himself that virtue had gone out of him, turned him about in the press, and said, Who touched my clothes? And his disciples said unto him, Thou seest the multitude thronging thee, and sayest thou, Who touched me? And he looked round about her to see her that had done this thing.*

*But the woman fearing and trembling, knowing what was done in her, came and fell down before him, and told him all the truth. And he said unto*

*her, Daughter, thy faith hath made thee whole; go in peace, and be whole of thy plague" (Mark 5: 25-34).*

This faithful woman was healed merely by touching Jesus' clothes. Jesus knew that virtue had gone out of Him because He felt the transfer of grace and power from Himself to this woman. When His grace entered her body, it transmuted and healed her body. Just by touching Jesus' clothing, this woman experienced transformation.

Jesus Christ is willing to do this for you. He is willing to elevate everything in your life that you are willing to offer to Him. Repentance is the process by which you willingly bring some aspect of your life to Jesus Christ and ask Him to transmute it and elevate it. When you do that, He *always* responds and *always* elevates whatever you have given Him. The more you repent, the more your capacity to receive grace from Jesus Christ will grow. The only prerequisite is that you must choose to repent; you much use your agency to make that choice. You must choose to come to Him and ask Him to change something for you. This requires your willingness to let go of the old patterns and emotions. Christ will not change the patterns in your life without your express participation and agreement because He honors your agency. Your participation in the process is necessary because the more conscious you are of those patterns that are holding you back—your thoughts, emotions, and past experiences—the faster you will be able to change them with Jesus Christ. Your awareness and participation both facilitate and accelerate your growth. You cannot repent of something that you are not aware of.

## The Repentance Process

So how do you do repent? How do you bring some-thing to Jesus Christ to be changed? The scriptures say: "By this ye may know if a man repenteth of his sins—behold, he will confess them and forsake them" (Doctrine and Covenants 58:43). Confessing and forsaking your sins means giving them to Jesus Christ. People tend to think of forsaking sins as not committing the sin anymore, but forsaking is really about surrendering. Your sins are pat-terns in your life that you cannot change on your own. Forsaking your sins means that you are ready to admit that you cannot change this on your own and that you desire to use your agency to ask for divine help. You are willing to surrender those sins (and anything undesir-able in your life) to Jesus Christ. After Christ purifies the energy and returns it to you, everything in your life will start to change. Your emotions, thoughts, and beliefs will change first, then your behavior and actions will start to change. Eventually, you will naturally let go of any unde-sirable patterns in your life as you consistently choose to engage in the repentance process.

Repentance is straightforward. A simple prayer or visualization is enough to bring in God's power. Here is an example of how you might use visualization to repent.

## Repentance Visualization

Go to a quiet, safe place where you can be alone and undisturbed. Say a quick prayer to begin the process. Tell God that you wish to repent of something. Ask for help and assistance with this process and ask God to bring you into balance as you repent. Take a few deep breaths to

calm your body and your mind. Be fully present with your repentance.

Close your eyes and visualize yourself in a beautiful, peaceful setting. You can visualize any place where you feel peaceful and comfortable. Visualize yourself in that setting, relaxed and calm.

Ask Jesus Christ to come and join you; visualize Him walking up to you. Trust that He is there with you. Remember that He always responds when you call upon Him, so He will be there. It is okay if you cannot visualize Him fully, just feel that He is there.

Think about the thing that you want to repent of. It can be anything: a difficult situation, something you feel guilty or ashamed about, something painful, or undesired emotions or thoughts. Express this burden to Jesus Christ in any way that feels comfortable to you. You can visualize yourself listing all the things you want to repent of. You can say the words aloud. You can write a list on paper. If you are feeling particularly emotional, then you can also express your emotions in any safe way that feels comfortable, such as hitting a pillow or crying. Continue to express what you want to turn over to Christ until you feel satisfied that you are finished.

Give your burden to Jesus Christ. Use your agency to choose to surrender it to Jesus Christ. You can do this in several ways. You can visualize yourself taking something out of your body or mind and walking over to Christ and handing it to Him. Or you can say the words "I choose to

give this to you." In some form or fashion, you must *choose* to surrender what is bothering you over to Christ.

Next, ask Christ to receive your offering and to purify and change it. Visualize Christ taking your offering and pulling it into Himself. Again, trust that He is doing this for you. He will never refuse you. He loves you and He loves your offering to Him. He delights in using His power to bless you. He does not judge you or your offering. Allow Him to receive what you are offering and to purify it for you.

Christ will then give you an offering in return. He might offer you a ball of light, or an object, or even a hug. Choose to reach out and to receive whatever Christ offers to you. He is returning the offering you gave to Him, but now it is in a purified form. You might even say the words "I choose to receive Christ's offering to me." This pure gift has the ability to elevate and change you for the better, but you must choose to receive it first.

Take a few deep breaths and notice how you feel. Allow gratitude to come into your heart. Thank Jesus Christ for helping you and thank God for this experience. Keep breathing deeply until you feel complete.

This is the repentance process. You have confessed your sins to Christ by telling Him what you desire to have changed in your life. You forsake sins by turning them over to Him completely. In the moment that you repent, you become one with Jesus Christ. Your offering becomes one with Jesus Christ. Jesus' offering back to you becomes one with you when you receive it. You are completely

unified with Jesus Christ in that moment. You are using His atonement for an *"at-one-ment"* moment—a moment of pure Oneness. It is a beautiful and a joyful process.

Jesus has said: "Behold, he who has repented of his sins, the same is forgiven, and I, the Lord, remember them no more" (Doctrine and Covenants 58:42). This is why receiving Christ's offering back to you is a critical component of the repentance process. Forgiveness of sins comes as you receive Christ's offering back into yourself. Your sins are forgiven because they are replaced with something better, an elevated version of what you surrendered. Whatever offering Christ gives to you is enveloped in His great, incomprehensible love for you. His offering often encompasses specific gifts to help you on your path, to assist you in your creations, and to help you let go of undesired patterns in your life. Repentance is a process, not a one-time fix all. Your engrained beliefs and patterns often have many layers to them, and it might take many iterations of the repentance process to remove all of those layers. As you continually surrender each layer to Christ, the heaviness of the sin decreases. You become elevated more and more until that sinful pattern has been completely purged from your life.

There might be times when it is difficult for you to receive what Christ is offering to you in this repentance visualization. Sometimes what Christ offers to you is so wonderful and glorious that you do not feel worthy of it. If you get stuck during the visualization and feel any resistance to receiving Christ's offering, then you need to get back into balance so you can receive it. Pray for balance and the ability to receive Christ's gift of grace. If you are feeling unworthiness or fear, you can go through the

repentance process for those emotions and resolve them so that you can receive Christ's offering. *Repentance is not complete until you have received Jesus Christ's gift for you.* That gift is Jesus Christ's grace. It is what changes you; you created space for it in your life by choosing to surrender your old patterns to Christ. It is critical that you stay engaged with the repentance process until you have fully received that gift.

The full steps of the repentance process outlined above might be necessary when you are feeling really stuck. It is also okay to shortcut some of these steps and repent quickly throughout the day. The two most important parts of this process are choosing to give something to Christ and then choosing to receive what He offers back to you. Both of these exchanges must take place and both of them must be received. You ensure that they both happen by using your agency to choose it. Just focus on making sure that those two exchanges have taken place. You can repent anywhere, anytime. It does not need to be a long, formal process, but take the time to do the visualization when you feel that you need extra help.

Remember that repentance is a straightforward process. We recognize, however, that there might be times when you feel that repentance is difficult or challenging. As we mentioned earlier, you cannot repent of something until you are aware of it. The process of becoming aware of the painful things in your life and what you feel and think about them can be very uncomfortable. It takes a lot of courage to look at yourself that deeply. While it is simple, there may be times that repentance feels uncomfortable. That is okay. Accept the discomfort and pray for the strength and courage to step into it. Trust that Jesus

Christ will change your pain and discomfort into peace and joy.

## Repentance Is About Surrender

Repentance is a process of surrender. Surrendering means yielding power and control over to someone else—to God in this case. There are some things in your life that you cannot fix on your own, despite all of your energy and efforts. There might be some habits you cannot break or some obstacles that you cannot overcome. Perhaps you keep feeling overwhelmed or discouraged by the challenges of your life. You can spend a lifetime trying to fix these things on your own, but you will find that your efforts are not enough. As the scriptures say, "For by grace are ye saved through faith; and that not of yourselves: it is the gift of God" (Ephesians 2:8). If you want to be saved from those difficult challenges and obstacles in your life, you will need to turn to God. You will need to access a power greater than your own. Repentance gives you access to that power.

You may come to a point in your life where you feel discouraged and frustrated that you cannot change something you want to change in your life. For example, suppose you are completely addicted to sugar. Whenever anything in your life goes wrong, you binge on sweets. No matter how hard you try, you cannot seem to stay away from sweet foods. You might try different diets or different reward systems. You can stick with them for a time, but eventually you keep going back to the sugar. This is an addiction—a pattern in your life. It is something you need to make you feel better, because you are out of balance. No matter how angry you get at yourself for this behavior, you cannot seem to change it. That is because it is not within

your control. There are underlying wounds and issues that are causing this problem for you, and until those wounds are healed, you will not be able to overcome this. You can repent of eating too much sugar, and you can repent of being angry with yourself for doing so. You can repent of whatever painful situation made you crave the sugar in the first place. You can repent of everything that is part of that pattern. As you keep repenting, you will see that pattern change.

Your emotional triggers are good signposts to alert you to things in your life that need repentance. Emotional triggers are situations that elicit an extreme emotional response. For example, someone may cut you off while you are driving one day. When it happens, you become irate. You might shout or swear. You might even be tempted to follow the other driver and ram him with your car. Although it can be annoying to be cut off, getting into a rage over something that little is extreme. Your extreme reaction stems from other layers of anger within you connected to your past experiences—experiences that are still bothering you because you still feel a strong emotional charge when you think about them. This is a sign that you need to repent of something. As you repent of your road rage, other past experiences that made you angry might come into your mind. Repent of those situations too. Surrender it all to Jesus Christ. When you repent of that wound and the associated emotions and experiences, then Christ can heal that wound and give you peace. When that happens, drivers who cut you off will no longer send you into a rage because the underlying issue has been healed.

The immediate result of repentance is getting back into balance. You will feel lighter and more peaceful, joyful,

and thankful. Whenever you repent and accept Jesus Christ's gift back to you, you will feel balanced. However, that does not mean that you will not be triggered again or that an issue is completely gone. Sometimes once is all that it takes. Other times you will need to repent many, many times before you start to see things shifting in your life. You have layers and layers of wounds that need to be healed. You might only be ready to let one small portion of your wounds go at a time. Be patient with this process, and be patient with yourself. If you repent often enough, you will see changes in your life. There is no need to judge yourself if the process seems slow. Focus on staying in balance rather than looking for a specific change in your life. Repentance is a beautiful process and an opportunity for you to have a personal experience with Jesus Christ. Focus on enjoying your repentance time with Christ and savoring His saving and redeeming power in your life.

## You Can Repent of Anything

Amulek taught the Zoramites about the far-reaching consequences of Jesus Christ's atonement,

> *"For it is expedient that an atonement should be made; for according to the great plan of the Eternal God there must be an atonement made, or else all mankind must unavoidably perish; yea, all are hardened; yea, all are fallen and are lost, and must perish except it be through the atonement which it is expedient should be made. For it is expedient that there should be a great and last sacrifice; yea, not a sacrifice of man, neither of beast, neither of any manner of fowl; for it shall not be a human*

*sacrifice; but it must be an infinite and eternal sacrifice" (Alma 34:9–10)*

Jesus Christ's atoning sacrifice is infinite and eternal, which means that it covers absolutely everything—every person, in every time, in every place.

This means that you are not limited to repenting for things that appear in your current physical reality. You can repent for situations that happened in the past—something you did that you feel guilty for, something that someone else did to hurt you, or just situations that didn't go in your favor and caused you to feel hurt, angry, or afraid. You can repent for all of that. You can repent of things you did in your pre-mortal life. You can even repent of the future by clearing out the doubts and fears that stand in the way of your creations. Anything in your life that you want to remove, purify, enhance, or strengthen can be surrendered through the repentance process. You can literally surrender anything in your life to Christ, and He can purify it. In fact, the process of becoming like God is the process of using Jesus Christ's atonement to purify every aspect of your life. As you do so, Jesus will take away the sting and pain from the past. When you allow Christ to purify the energy from your past and you receive His offering to you, those effects ripple into your present state. Consistent repentance can change your whole life.

Now this is where things get really exciting. The beauty of this process is that repentance does not just apply to your sins or unwanted patterns, but to everything in your life. Jesus Christ can make bad things good and good things better. Through the repentance process, you can even give to Christ the things that you love in your

life and He will make them even more incredible. Jesus Christ can elevate *all* things. Whatever you give to Christ comes back to you elevated and multiplied. Christ makes amazing deals with people. He says to you, "Give me a dollar, and I will give you $100." He takes any meager offering you give and multiplies it exponentially. He will do that for anything in your life! So why wouldn't you want to repent for everything all the time?

## Becky's Story About Applying Repentance to Dating

One of the most painful things in my life has been my experiences with dating. For most of my life, dating meant rejection. It was hard to get a date, and first dates never seemed to turn into second dates. I would attend singles' activities and felt like the men there would barely acknowledge my existence, let alone show any interest in me. I would rarely get asked to dance when I showed up at dances. It was very discouraging, and I was constantly wondering what was wrong with me. I didn't want to give up on my hope of finding someone, so I kept trying and kept putting myself out there. I read dating advice blogs and worked on getting better at flirting. But nothing seemed to change.

I prayed often for help from God. As I shared in my story in the Introduction, God led me on a path of learning that started with a class on mindfulness. I was directed to read books, take classes, talk to mentors, and seek for greater truth in a variety of places. I learned that the way to have better dating experiences was to seek more healing from Jesus Christ. For years, God was trying to communicate to me through my dating experiences. He was trying to show me pain from the past that I was holding on to. I

realized that I believed many things about myself, about men, and about dating that did not represent God's truth. I believed that I was unattractive and unlovable. I believed that men were shallow jerks. I believed that I would never find someone and that I wasn't worthy of love. I believed that I was not good at dating. I thought my bad dating experiences were proof that those beliefs were true. In actuality, God was just trying to show me those beliefs so that I would choose to repent of them and receive new beliefs.

Sometime after I had started learning that the painful experiences in my life could show me what I needed to repent of, I attend a singles' dance. These dances were not my favorite activity, but I had a couple friends to go with and wanted to make an effort. I bought a new dress that I looked good in, and I went to the dance with high hopes. I was outgoing and friendly and talked to a lot of people. I danced often. But that whole night, not one single man asked me to dance with him. The DJ played plenty of slow songs, but I sat them out. It was a triggering experience. I judged myself and everyone else. I was frustrated that all of the men flocked to a few women and didn't pay attention to the rest of us. I felt embarrassed and ashamed. In the past, I would have let an experience like this get me really down, and I would use it as an excuse to skip out on singles' activities in the future. This time, I used it as an opportunity to take a closer look at my wounds and belief systems instead. I spent some time in prayer discussing my experience with God and sharing my pain with Him. I told God how it made me feel, and I shared with Him experiences from my past where I felt wounded by how men treated me or ignored me. I took a close look

at what I believed—that I was unlovable and undesirable. I chose to repent of those beliefs and all of these undesirable experiences.

For me, these patterns were pretty deep-rooted, so I had to repent of them many times. I kept trying to date and attend singles' activities. I knew that if I was triggered by what I experienced at those activities, that it was a gift. It showed me the next thing that I needed to surrender to Jesus Christ. As I did that, I started to open myself up to think about dating in a new way. I felt impressed to try some different online dating sites that I had not been open to before. It was satisfying to see how over the span of a several years, my dating experiences got better and better. I was meeting more men that I was interested in, and I was having better conversations with them. Men started to be more complimentary to me. I started enjoying flirting and dating much more. There were times that I would take a break from dating to focus more on my personal healing, but every time I jumped back into the dating scene, my experiences were noticeably better. I remember the first time that a man looked me in the eyes and told me that I am beautiful. I was 43 years old. That was a turning point for me, and I knew that my repentance process was working.

I met my boyfriend, Kennard, through on online dating site. I had started dating someone else soon after I met him, but we remained friends and would email each other from time to time. After my other relationship ended, our friendship continued to grow and develop. We connected easily with each other. After a couple years, I realized that I didn't want to date anyone else. I just wanted to date Kennard. I wasn't meeting anyone that I could

connect with as much as I did with him. Kennard and I are amazed at the way that God brought us together. We fit so well together despite having significantly different backgrounds. I am an educated, middle class white woman and he is a black man who grew up in an inner-city environment. Yet we share many of the same interests, values, and goals. We are enjoying a loving relationship, and I am excited to see where it leads me.

I would never have gotten to this point without really learning how to repent and learning to see how to apply repentance to the discouraging experiences in my life. I had to learn that I wouldn't get a boyfriend by enduring miserable experiences and begging God for something different. I needed to use those experiences to seek greater healing through repentance. I stopped being afraid of triggering, painful experiences. While I didn't necessarily like those experiences, I understood how they were helping me. I used them to identify and understand what patterns and beliefs I needed to repent of. I loved that I had something proactive that I could do to help me move toward what I desired. I could repent and forgive and allow God to restore me to peace. Those powerful tools changed my life.

Repentance is an important tool to help you stay in balance, particularly when you feel stuck in a certain problem or pattern. Pay attention to your thoughts and emotions. When you are fixated on a particular issue or feeling a strong, recurring emotion, that is a good signal

that it is time to repent. Repentance will elevate you and will start shifting everything in your life. Repent every day. Repent of everything. It brings Christ great joy when you use His atonement. He greatly desires to bless you and to change your life, but He can only do so when you choose to surrender through repentance. Repentance takes the full use of your agency. Whenever your life feels chaotic or if a prayer does not feel like enough to get you back into balance, take a few minutes to repent and have a personal experience with Jesus Christ. He will restore you to a balanced state with God and make it easier for you to maintain that balance.

# Chapter 6
## Forgiveness

Forgiveness is another important tool to help return you to a balanced state. Like repentance, forgiveness helps release you from the negative thoughts, emotions, and experiences that make it difficult for you to stay balanced. Consistent forgiveness will change and transform you, just like repentance. Forgiveness is powerful because it helps to dislodge the old patterns that you are trying to overcome. It is a profound way to exercise your agency. Before we discuss forgiveness, however, we need to discuss judgment and how judgment pulls you out of balance.

### The Problem With Judgment

A judgment is a belief you have about someone or something. Because your judgments are beliefs—and are often based on unconscious biases and limited experiences—they are not always accurate. You often make negative judgments about people or things when your experience with them leads to unwanted emotions, like sadness or anger. For example, you might meet a new person at church. That person might not seem responsive to your

attempts to talk to him. You feel hurt and embarrassed that you reached out to this stranger and got a lukewarm response. You judge that man as being cold and unfriendly, perhaps even unlikeable. That is a negative judgment. While that judgment may feel true as it relates to that particular experience, that man might not actually be a cold and unfriendly person. He might just be shy and fearful. Whatever the case, your judgment of that man will affect how you act around and toward him.

The problem with negative judgments is that they pull you out of balance. Whenever you see that man, you will remember how hurt you felt when he was not friendly to you and that hurt can pull you out of balance. In some situations, your judgements will be even more negative because your emotions around the event or situation were even stronger. Judgement acts as a shackle that keeps you chained to the painful situation, the negative emotions associated with it, and the person that you blame for the situation. This is why you keep processing and reprocessing a painful situation in your mind—because you have created a chain to bind you to that situation through your judgment. This is why Christ has urged: "Judge not, that ye be not judged. For with what judgment ye judge, ye shall be judged: and with what measure ye mete, it shall be measured to you again" (Matthew 7:1–2). In this scripture, Jesus is teaching about this chain of judgement. He is telling you that when you judge, you are stuck with whatever judgment you made. You will keep reliving that painful experience. When you feel a strong negative emotion toward a person or situation that you have judged, then you know you are shackled in the chain of judgment.

You have probably had experiences in your life that have brought you pain, shame, sorrow, fear, or anger. In those circumstances, it is human nature to look for someone or something to blame for your pain, including yourself. Blame itself is a negative judgement; you are judging someone or something as causing you pain. It does not matter whether the other person is really responsible or not—what matters is that the assignment of blame is a negative judgment that has consequences for *your* life. Blame will always pull you out of balance and disturb *your* peace. Even when the blame is totally deserved, that act of blaming will unbalance you. Blame will also keep you chained to that particular situation, person, or problem and force you to relive it.

This is why judgment is so powerful and so harmful. Judgment robs you of peace by disturbing your balance with God. The more aware you are of the judgments you make throughout the day, the more you will be able to stay in balance. You can repent of any judgment that you make. Forgiveness is another tool to restore your balance. When you forgive the people in your life that you blame or the situations that cause you pain, you break the chain keeping you tethered to the pain associated with that person or situation.

## What Is Forgiveness?

Forgiveness is the process of breaking the chain between yourself and an undesirable situation and allowing the situation to be healed and to fade from your life. Forgiveness means to "cease to feel resentment against (an offender)."[9] You activate forgiveness through your agency.

---

[9] https://www.merriam-webster.com/dictionary/forgive

While some of your resentments may diminish with time, real forgiveness must be conscious and intentional in order to heal the negative emotions associated with the situation. Forgiveness is the act of choosing to remove a negative judgment or release someone from blame.

In order to initiate the forgiveness process, all you have to do is say that you forgive something. It is truly that simple. It is important to forgive all aspects of the situation—yourself for casting the judgement, the judgment itself, and the other person or thing that you have judged. For example, your brother may have said something hurtful to you, which causes you to judge him as insensitive and selfish. In order to activate forgiveness, you would say: "I choose to forgive myself for judging my brother. I choose to forgive my judgment of insensitivity and selfishness. I choose to forgive my brother for saying what he said to me." You can say the words aloud or in your mind, depending on what feels more comfortable to you.

You do not need to feel completely softhearted toward a person or situation in order to forgive. A desire to forgive is sufficient. You merely have to be willing to use your agency to move in the direction of shifting the judgment. If you are not feeling particularly forgiving, you can still say the words "I forgive you" and let that powerful statement start to break the chains binding you. Your only responsibility is to activate your agency to forgive. When you do so, you bring God's power in your life. You might have to forgive the person or situation many times in order to fully emotionally free yourself from that situation, but the consistent exercise of your agency in activating

forgiveness will eventually break those chains. You only need to be willing.

It is important to emphasize that forgiveness does not mean that you excuse, condone, or pardon those things that someone has done to hurt you. It does not mean that the other person is in the right or even that they should not be subject to the consequences of their behavior. Forgiveness is not meant for them. It is meant for you! Forgiveness is what will set *you* free from the situation and all the pain it caused you. You know that you are done forgiving someone when all of those negative judgments and feelings are gone. When you have completely forgiven, you can stand in the same room with someone who has hurt you and feel nothing but complete love for them and for yourself. That is how you know when you are done forgiving. Until you arrive at that point, keep forgiving that person or situation. Every time you do so, you shift how you feel about it.

If your choices or someone else's choices produced consequences that are still bothering you, you can repent of that situation. You merely need to surrender all those consequences and everything that bothers you about the situation through the repentance process and ask Christ to transmute and purify it all for you. Forgiveness and repentance work perfectly together. You can even make it a practice to forgive everything before you surrender it to Christ. That will increase your capacity to receive Christ's gift to you in return.

Choose to forgive anything in your life that is causing you any pain or angst. Many people find that it is hardest to forgive themselves for things that they have done or said. It is important for you to forgive yourself because

that is part of the process of removing the chains binding you to your past negative experiences and to who you were in the past. If you desire for Christ to turn you into a new person, you must first forgive who you were. If you find it hard to forgive yourself, then forgive yourself for making it so hard. The more loving and forgiving to yourself you are, the faster things will shift in your life. When your heart is closed against yourself, it will be difficult for you to receive Jesus Christ's gift to you in the repentance process. Keep your heart open through constant forgiveness.

## Forgiveness and Repentance Work Together

Forgiveness and repentance work together in harmony to free you from those things that are difficult and painful—both in the present and in your past. Remember that your judgments act as chains that keep you bound to anything that you judge, including people, experiences, and possessions. Those things that you judge become your burdens, such as a painful experience from the past, a difficult coworker, a child who is struggling at school, or a pain in your body. Your judgements keep you chained to these undesirable situations and all of the unwanted emotions like pain, fear, anger, and grief that are associated with them. The more you judge, the more your life looks like the person shown in the first panel of Figure 3—an unhappy individual who is chained to many heavy burdens.

CHAINS:
your judgements

WEIGHTS:
- wounds
- stuck emotions
- past painful experiences
- challenging relationships

FORGIVENESS: removes the chains
(unshackles you)

REPENTANCE

completely dissolves
the weights & chains—
one layer at a time.

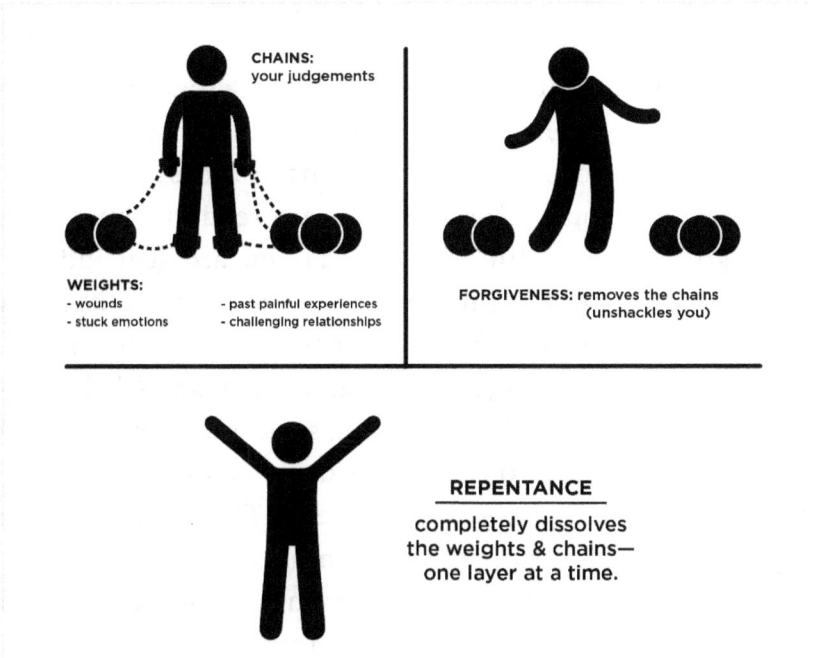

**Figure 3: Forgiveness and Repentance Remove the
Chains and Weights**

When you choose to forgive, you remove those chains. The burdens may still be there, but they aren't pulling on you and weighing you down. You feel free and peaceful because you choose to remove those chains (judgments). This is shown in the second panel of Figure 3. However, those weights that you were fastened to are still part of your reality. If you desire for those weights to be removed completely from your life to create space for something new and better, then repent. You can repent of each one of those situations, wounds, or experiences that you previously judged. As you surrender each one to Jesus Christ through repentance, He will purify and transmute that situation or experience. As each wound is healed, it dissolves the chain and the weight associated with it. This opens up

more space in your life to receive better experiences and situations from God.

Repentance and forgiveness work together. Both require your agency and your willing participation. Forgiveness speeds up the repentance process because it unchains you and shows that you are ready to let something go from your life. As long as you are still judging someone or something in your life, then you are keeping yourself chained to it. You can still repent of that situation and receive something better from Jesus Christ. As long as you are still judging that situation, you are still choosing to hold on to that experience in some small way. You are only giving *some* of it to Jesus Christ, but not *all* of it. This will slow down the repentance process and your personal healing because you are only giving up a small portion of your burden at a time rather than the whole thing. Forgiveness accelerates the benefits you receive from repentance.

Forgiveness helps you to achieve and maintain balance. Forgiveness is particularly powerful when you use it in conjunction with repentance. Sometimes the chains that keep you bound to unwanted sin, baggage, or patterns are strong and you cannot just surrender them to the Savior. Forgiveness breaks the chains so that you are then free to give your offering to Christ through repentance. Both processes bring God's power into your life. Both change you in positive ways. The more you access and use the power of forgiveness in your life, the more you will become like

God. You will see yourself, others, and your life more clearly, because you have chosen to release judgment and blame through forgiveness. You will feel more gratitude, love, and joy.

Achieving and maintaining your balance with God is crucial if you want to create the life you desire. Stay aware throughout the day of how you are doing emotionally, mentally, and physically. Your emotions, thoughts, and sensations of your body are important clues to help you recognize when you are not in balance. A simple prayer or longer visualization are enough to restore you to balance when you need it. However, if you are struggling to stay in balance, repent of any challenging situations or emotions that are pulling you out of balance. Forgive yourself, others, and everything in your life. Consistent repentance and forgiveness will make it easier for you to stay in balance throughout the day. They are gifts from God to help you to change your nature and to shift everything in your life in a positive direction. The better you are at staying in balance, the easier and faster the creation process will go. In the next section, we discuss the creation process. We will teach you how you can use hope, faith, and charity to create a life you love. Balance with God is a critical component of that process, and repentance and forgiveness are crucial processes to help you stay in balance.

# Part 2:
## The Creation Process

# Chapter 7
## The Framework for Creation

The overarching purpose of this book is to teach you how to fully partner with God so that you can create what you desire—the experiences, relationships, situations, and possessions that will bring you joy, fulfillment, and peace. To do this, you must understand the principles of hope, faith, and charity and know how to put them into practice.

Hope, faith, and charity are incredibly powerful tools, which is why the scriptures talk so much about these topics. They are godly principles, meaning that they are fully aligned with God's purposes and power. Hope, faith, and charity need to be used together in unity. The prophet Mormon discussed this:

*"And again, my beloved brethren, I would speak unto you concerning hope. How is it that ye can attain unto faith, save ye shall have hope?*

*Wherefore, if a man have faith he must needs have hope; for without faith there cannot be any hope.*

*And again, behold I say unto you that he cannot
have faith and hope, save he shall be meek and
lowly of heart....and if a man be meek and lowly in
heart...he must needs have charity; for if he have
not charity he is nothing; wherefore he must needs
have charity"* (Moroni 7:40, 42–44).

Mormon is explaining that faith, hope, and charity work
together. There is no faith without first having hope, but
without faith, the hope cannot exist. You cannot have one
without the other. They are completely intertwined and
interconnected. Faith and hope also do not work without
charity. Faith and hope need the power of charity to be
effective. They all build upon each other.

It is not enough to know that these three virtues are
important and connected to each other. You must understand the role that each virtue plays in the creation process.
This enables you to identify when one is lacking and to
take steps to bring more of that power into your creation.
Without a clear understanding of how to use hope, faith,
and charity together, you will not be able to fully activate
their power. The framework for creation outlines the roles
that hope, faith, and charity play in the creation process.

## The Framework for Creation

The framework for creation is straightforward. The
creation process involves three main components: hope,
faith, and charity. We view these as tools to help you
understand what you and God each contribute to the creation process. Hope, faith, and charity guide your actions
and enhance your power to create. You complete the creation process by resting in God—a state of opening yourself up to receive what you have created. When you use

these tools together with a good understanding of how they contribute to creation, you will be able to create what you desire for your life.

Creation begins and ends with hope. We define your "hope" as the thing that you desire for your life. This hope might be intangible, such as a more harmonious relationship, greater financial abundance, or better health. Your hope might be something tangible, such as a new car, a bigger house, or a trip to Tahiti. Your hope is your desired end goal for the creation process. The creation process begins when you focus on one of your hopes and choose to apply these tools to create that hope with God. When you choose to create your hope, your agency sets everything in motion by activating the spiritual creation of what you desire. Then you must surrender that hope to God, meaning that instead of trying to force the outcome, you allow God to oversee the creation process.

Faith is the principle guiding your actions. Keep in mind that these actions will likely not be what you think they *should* be. Your responsibility is to take only inspired action—actions that are revealed to you in the moment, often in the form of an impulse or desire. You will feel in your heart when you are supposed to do something. You will not know what these steps are ahead of time; they come to you one at a time in the correct order and sequence. That is where the faith comes in. You trust that God is leading you to your hope and that He is inspiring your footsteps. Faith is complete confidence in God's guidance and help even though you do not have any evidence that your hope is any closer to you. Faith is surrendering control and not trying to make your hope appear by

checking items off your to-do list or staying busy trying to create what you desire on your own.

Faith dictates what actions you need to take to create your hope. Some of your most important actions are repentance and forgiveness. Repentance and forgiveness are essential to creation because they help you to remove the judgments, beliefs, emotions, and trauma that pull you out of balance and prevent you from receiving your hope. There might be times when you hit road bumps in the process, get discouraged about how long it is taking, or worry that the process is not working. Those moments are gifts because they show you the judgments, beliefs, and emotions that are not consistent with your desired outcome. Through repentance and forgiveness, God can remove those blocks and change your nature so that you have the capacity to receive your hope. Repentance and forgiveness help you stay balanced with God throughout the whole creation process.

You allow God to direct creation by staying in balance. When you are balanced with God, you allow God's full power to operate in your life. God's power is charity—a love so pure, divine, and strong that it transforms everything it touches. When you are balanced, God's power—charity—will touch and transform every step of the creation process. Charity ensures that all of the pieces come together in the best way. Charity provides you with inspiration about what you need to do and the peace to be content during those times when you do not need to take any action. It ensures that everything happens in the gentlest, smoothest, fastest way possible. Staying in balance allows you and your hope to be enveloped in charity, which is the perfect state for exercising your faith.

The final part of the creation process is resting in God. God rested after creating the Earth, and you must rest at various stages throughout this process. Resting is a state of receiving—a state where you open yourself up to receive what you have created. Resting also helps you to stay balanced throughout the process. It helps you to disconnect from doing and focus on being connected to God.

## An Illustration of the Creation Process

Figure 4 depicts a metaphor for how hope, faith, and charity work together in the creation process. In this metaphor, you are in in a boat, and you desire to sail to a distant island. That island is your hope—your end goal that you desire to create. You hope to get your boat to that shore.

**CHARITY = THE WIND**

**YOUR HOPE**

**FAITH =** USING SAIL TO CATCH THE WIND
NOT CONTROLLING MOMENTUM OR DIRECTION

**Figure 4: An Illustration of the Creation Process**

Your boat represents your faith. As an expression of faith, you leave your rudder on the shore; you will not be able to steer the boat. You surrender control and direction of the process to God. You also leave your oars on the shore because you do not want to try to force creation by trying to row to the island all by yourself. You are going to let God do the heavy work of getting you to your hope. The only action you can take with your boat is moving the sail to catch the wind. This represents your inspired action. You only need to move the sail when you can feel the wind changing. At first, it might seem that the wind is pushing you in the wrong direction or taking you on a longer route, but your faith allows you to trust that the wind will get you to your hope. You stay focused on catching that wind in your sails, not trying to steer or row the boat.

The wind is charity. It is present the entire journey and pushes you and your boat toward your hope. It navigates around any obstacles in your path. The wind is also blowing in the right direction for you, even if it does not seem like it. When you are balanced with God, you can easily catch that wind in your sail. When you are out of balance, you struggle to catch the wind with your sail and only inch forward on your journey. The more you focus on staying in balance with God, the faster your journey goes and the sooner you arrive at your hope.

As with any journey, your boat might have a few problems along the way. You might spring a leak or tear a sail. These obstacles represent any judgments, beliefs, or stuck emotions that are not consistent with your goal. This is where repentance and forgiveness come in. Repentance will mend your sail and patch the hole in your boat.

Forgiveness will bail out the water that came in through the hole, allowing your boat to travel much faster. Together, repentance and forgiveness allow you to overcome any problems that arise so you can focus on catching a strong wind in your sails and reaching that distant island.

Along the way, you have plenty of opportunities to sit back in your boat and rest. You allow God to direct the process and trust His timing. Instead of worrying about whether it is working and whether you are heading in the right direction, you focus on living fully in the present moment and enjoying the journey. You enjoy the beautiful scenery and the warmth of the sun on your face. You relax and enjoy the trip, trusting that the wind will get you to your hope.

## How Creation Works—Becky's Story of Creating a Raise

To show you how this works, I will share a time when I created something better for my life. Recently I felt discontented with my salary at work. I had worked as a faculty member at a public university for eight years without a substantial raise. I did not feel that I was getting paid what I deserved for the work that I was doing. My hope was to get a substantial raise. I desired to stay at my current university, but I knew that I needed to be open and let God deliver a bigger salary to me in the best way, not in my way. I opened myself up to the idea of moving somewhere else, but I told God that my desire was to stay at my current university.

A colleague at another university reached out to me and invited me to apply to an open position in his department. I felt impressed to put in the application, and I even

started getting excited about the possibilities of this new position. As I was waiting to hear back from the university about interviewing, I also felt a lot of fear about the potential moving. Would I be able to afford a house in this new area? Would I make friends? Would this be a better situation for me? As these fears arose, I would apply the repentance process and surrender them to Jesus Christ. I tried to focus on staying in balance.

I later found out that I was not going to be invited to do a campus interview at that university, and I was very disappointed. There were some unique circumstances around that rejection that led to me feeling very hurt and angry. Those feelings pulled me out of balance again. I allowed myself to acknowledge and feel those emotions, but I also repented of them and surrendered them to Christ. When I would get frustrated with myself for falling out of balance so often, I would forgive myself.

I learned about a position at a different university and applied for that job. I was invited for an on-campus interview. I felt that I did a good job in the interview and that I was a strong candidate for the position, but the decision-making process at that university was very slow. Over a month had gone by, and I still had not heard anything about that job. I received an email from a colleague at a third university who invited me to submit an application for an open position at his university.

While I was waiting, I focused on living in the present moment instead of wondering what would happen in the future. I sometimes wondered whether I would be moving that summer and where I would end up. I had no idea where I would be in a year, but I knew that I could not focus on the ambiguity and uncertainties of my situation.

Instead, I tried to be present with what I was doing and focus on staying in balance. I kept working at my job and going about my normal activities. I was helping with a program in another division on campus and told the other leaders that I was looking into other jobs and might not be there to help with the program the following year. The people running that program asked if there was anything they could do to help, and, on an impulse, I told them that they could have the vice president of their division write a letter to the dean of my school telling him to try to retain me at the university. To my surprise, they agreed to do so. Even more surprising, the vice president (who had only met me once a few years before) was willing to write the letter.

Immediately after receiving the letter, my dean contacted me to ask what it would take to keep me at my current university. We discussed what I wanted, particularly a substantial increase in salary. My dean said that he would ask the provost for funds to give me a salary increase, but that he would need some proof that I was serious about leaving the university. I shared with the dean the interview itinerary for the interview that I had already done and the letter inviting me to apply for the other open position.

Four days later, my dean reached out to me and offered me a substantial raise. The higher salary would be effective immediately instead of applying to the next academic year. While the salary was not as much as I had hoped, the dean added a few extra incentives into the package to make it worth my while. To me, it ended up being the best possible outcome. I got the raise I desired, and I was able to stay at my current university. I had created my hope.

As I reflected upon the process, I realized several things. First, the catalyst for me getting this raise was the letter from the vice president—something that I had asked for on a whim, an impulse of the moment. Second, if I had not done an interview at another university and been invited to apply at a second university, the dean would not have had the leverage that he needed to get funding from the provost to give me a raise. Third, I had to allow myself to change through this process. All of this unfolded over several months. There were many times during the process where I felt fearful, angry, disappointed, or impatient. I also felt like I was in limbo for several months, not knowing where I would be living the next year. Because of this, I had to spend months being very mindful of my emotions and using repentance and forgiveness to help me to stay in balance. I feel that by focusing on staying in balance, I was able to get the outcome I desired. The route to my hope was a bit circuitous and it came in an unexpected way, but that is how I know that God delivered it to me.

## How Creation Works—Lacey's Story About Creating Funding for Her Mission

One Sunday in 2006, I was at church singing the hymn "I'll Go Where You Want Me to Go" with the congregation. As I sang the hymn, I felt an impression that I would serve an 18-month mission for my church. The impression surprised me because I had never thought about serving a mission nor had a desire to do so. But as soon as I received that impression, the desire to serve a mission started to grow in my heart.

At the time, I was dating an incredible guy who was going to leave shortly to serve a mission himself. I had been half-heartedly trying to break things off with him for several months because he was going to be gone for two years. But I was so in love with him that I just couldn't follow through with it. After receiving this impression at church, I went to his house and told him about my new-found desire to serve a mission. I was nervous about how he might react, so I was shocked when he lit up at hearing my idea. He thought it was a great idea, especially because I would not be dating anyone while I served my mission, and he hoped that we would get married when our missions were complete. His excitement over the idea of me serving a mission made me desire it even more. It felt like the right thing for me to do, and I started getting excited about it.

I prayed and told God that I had chosen to serve a mission. I asked God to set everything up for me and to provide a way for me to go. Then I chose to proceed with my preparations and leave the rest to God.

I started by telling my parents of my desire to serve a mission. They didn't really think that I was serious about it. They thought I was only doing it because the guy I was dating wanted me to, and they thought that my desire would wane in a few months. But I jumped wholeheart-edly into my preparations. I had a brother who was also preparing to serve a mission, so we were able to work on our preparations together. We submitted our applications for our missions at the same time and recieved our mission assignments the same day. Our whole extended family turned out to celebrate the news with us. It was such a joyful time for me.

About a month after I learned about my mission assignment, my father asked to talk to me. He had been going through the family finances and was concerned. He wanted to know how serious I was about serving a mission. I told him that I was very serious and that I planned to go. He said that he and my mother had not expected me to want to serve a mission. They didn't have enough money to send two children on a mission, and they felt that the money they had saved should be used to support my brother who had always wanted to serve. I was stunned and didn't know what to say. With tears in my eyes, I told my dad that I was going to serve a mission and that God would provide a way for me to do so.

Immediately after that conversation, I went to my room, full of emotion. I prayed and asked God to confirm whether my hope to serve a mission was the right thing for me. I felt an immediate sense of peace and knew this was the right step for me. I felt a desire to pray for a financial miracle and ask that God would provide the funds for my mission. I asked God to do this in such a way that my parents and I would know that it was God who provided for us.

Then the miracles started. My grandfather, who did not affiliate with our church, decided to donate money to help fund both my brother's mission and mine. An older couple who lived by us came over one evening and donated $1,000 toward each of our missions. I was moved with gratitude and joy! I knew that God was helping me, but I was still $6,000 short of what I needed for my mission.

About a week later, I received a call from an insurance agent. He wanted to talk to me about a car accident that I had been in the previous year with my mother. The

prior January, my mom had driven to pick me up from college so that I could come home for the weekend. We were driving through a mountain pass and hit some black ice. The car swerved out of control, spun around, flipped upside down, and crashed into the side of the mountain. The windshield caved in and the car was half buried in rocks and dirt. Miraculously, my mom and I both survived the crash. Some kind passersby helped us get to a hospital. First responders were amazed that we had survived.

The insurance agent was now telling me that we had not received all of the treatments that we were entitled to as part of that accident. They wanted to make things right so that we would not come back later and sue them for their negligence. They told me that they were sending me a check in the mail that week to cover this discrepancy. When the letter arrived and I looked at the check, I started to cry. The check was for $6,000—exactly what I needed to finish funding my mission. I knew without a doubt that God had provided this to me and that months before my mission He had prepared a way to finance it.

The sweet details of this hope are what makes working with God so perfect. The detail that the guy I was in love with was inspiring me and encouraging me. The detail of having my brother by my side going through the preparation with me. The detail of knowing God prepared a way for the money to be there even before I developed the hope to serve a mission. To top it off, I arrived home from my mission the same day as the young man I had been dating arrived home from his mission—and we did end up marrying each other! All of these miraculous and perfectly orchestrated details were brought about not just for my good, but for my joy! That is just how God works.

## Creation Is About Changing Yourself

God is the ultimate Creator. He is constantly creating new worlds and beings of all kinds to populate them. God desires that you also experience the joy of creating the desires of your heart. God desires for you to progress and become a goddess or god yourself, which means that you need to learn to create. The creation tools in this book can have a powerful and profound impact on your personal growth, learning, and progression because the whole process is about changing yourself with God's help and support. Creation is about healing any wounds in your life that prevent you from being fully unified with God and that prevent what you desire from coming into your life.

As you apply these creation tools, you will become a new person. You will be in tune with the desires of your heart. You will claim your agency. You will be able to surrender your life to God. You will be less stressed and more relaxed because you trust this process. You will become a person who spends more time in balance with God, which means that you will experience more peace, joy, love, and contentment. You will become a person who is proficient at repentance and forgiveness and who is free from the burdens of the past. As you change, you will feel closer to God. You will feel your own power grow. The more you create, the more you will become like God.

The laws and rules that surround creation are universal, which means that anyone can use and apply them irrespective of what that person desires to create and why. The laws governing creation are not respecters of persons, and they do not judge your desires. They simple obey your commands. This is why you sometimes create undesirable things in your life. You are creating all the time, and if

you are not intentional about using these tools to create what you desire, you might unconsciously create what you do not desire. In particular, the more time you spend out of balance, the more you will mis-create, meaning that your creations will be distorted or undesirable. When you stay in balance, apply these tools of creation, and work in harmony with them, you will create many beautiful and enjoyable things for your life.

Becoming a master creator will take practice; it is a learning process. As you work on applying these tools, do not be afraid of doing something wrong. That fear will pull you out of balance with God and interfere with your ability to create. God will lead you through this process. Even if you were to create a "mistake," or something that you judge as undesirable, God will use that as an opportunity to teach you more about yourself and more about the creation process. He will reveal to you those judgments and beliefs that are preventing your hope from coming into your life. With this knowledge, you can repent and change those beliefs and get the creation process working smoothly again. Remember that your most important work in the creation process is staying balanced and connected with God.

It will take some time to learn to create effectively. The physical realm is governed by the construct of time, so physical processes and physical creations are subject to time. There might be times when your hopes manifest quickly and other times when they take longer. The timing of receiving your hopes is outside of your control. Choose to be okay with the fact that creation is an iterative process that takes some time. Know that it will take some practice

before you are proficient at creation. Choose to trust yourself, trust the process, and trust God.

Now that you know the general framework for creation, we will explain each element of the creation process in more detail. The following chapters provide a more detailed explanation of each of the main elements of the creation process: hope, faith, charity, and rest. The more you understand these concepts and the creative power they represent, the more successful you will be at creating your desires.

# Chapter 8
## Hope

Creation starts with hope—a desire for something better. That hope jumpstarts the creation process by establishing the end goal for the process. All you need is an idea—a spark—of something you would like to have in your life. However, you must also nurture that desire by giving yourself permission to want it without any judgment. Hoping is thinking about what you desire, visualizing what your life will look like when that desire manifests, and allowing yourself to feel joyful and excited at the prospect. That excitement will inspire the creation of your hope.

### What Is Hope?

The dictionary provides several interesting definitions of hope:

> (1) *"cherish a desire with anticipation, to want something to happen or be true"*

> (2) *"desire with expectation of obtainment or fulfillment"*

*(3) "expect with confidence."* [10]

According to these definitions, your hopes are your cherished desires—what you really want to have or experience. Remember that this desire can be a state of being, an event, or a tangible object. Your hope, or the thing you desire to have or experience, is your intended outcome for the creation process.

A hope is different from a goal. A goal is an outcome that you expect to achieve through your own efforts. A hope is something you desire that is not completely within your control. This distinction is important because it affects your attitudes and actions in the creation process. If you treat your hope like a goal, you will spend your time trying to control every aspect of the process, which can block or slow down creation. While there are many wonderful and desirable goals that you can achieve through your efforts alone, that is not the focus of this book. Instead, our desire is to teach you how to partner with God so you can create your hope through God's power rather than your own. You do not receive your hope by working hard; it is hand-delivered to you by God. Goals are things you work to achieve. Hopes, on the other hand, arrive through faith and charity.

These definitions of hope also indicate that hope is having confidence that your desire will be fulfilled. One way to learn about hope is to remember the feeling of anticipating Christmas Day when you were a child. As a child, every day leading up to Christmas was filled with the anticipation of wonderful things—presents, treats, fun with family and friends, new experiences. You might have

---

[10] https://www.merriam-webster.com/dictionary/hope

been so excited about Christmas morning that you would wake up hours earlier than usual because you were excited about opening your presents and seeing what you would receive. This feeling of positive, eager anticipation is part of hope. It is knowing what you desire and believing that you will receive it.

When you base your hope on a perceived need rather than a desire, it can create feelings of desperation, control, anxiety, or fear. When you feel that you need something in order to be safe or happy, then it is easy for you to spend time worrying about whether or not you will get that thing, leading to more effort to control everything. This can derail or degrade the creation process and lead to less desirable outcomes. Hope operates best on desire because your desires are more likely to be accompanied with joy, peace, and other emotions that support the creation process.

## The Emotional and Mental Components of Hope

In the creation process, hope pertains to the spiritual creation of the thing you desire. Remember the scripture we quoted earlier: "For I, the Lord God, created all things, of which I have spoken, spiritually, before they were naturally upon the face of the earth" (Moses 3:5). Everything must be created spiritually before it can be created physically. This is also true in the creation process we discuss here. You use your mind to envision your hope, you fill that vision with positive emotions, and then you use your agency to choose it. Agency activates spiritual creation and hope gives it direction. The process starts with feeling excited about creating something and then getting a clear picture of what you desire.

The emotional component of hope is allowing yourself to feel what it would be like to have your hope in your life. For example, suppose you really want a new car. Sit and think for a moment about what it would feel like to have that car. Feel the joy associated with receiving that car. Feel the gratitude of driving around in your new car. Be excited about it. Feel your love for this new car. It is not enough to list the emotions that you will have when you get that car—you must *feel* the emotions. One way to know if you are feeling those emotions is to pay attention to what your body wants to do. You express your emotions through your body, so there is always a physical impulse accompanying each emotion. Follow those impulses. Maybe you feel so happy that you want to throw your arms into the air. Perhaps you feel so much gratitude that you want to cry. You might even feel so excited that you start dancing or jumping into the air. Allow yourself to wave your arms, cry, or jump up and down. Following the impulses of your body will help you to feel the emotions associated with receiving your hope.

These emotions are crucial. Your joy, gratitude, and excitement are evidence that your creation is being fueled by charity. The stronger those emotions and the more you can hold onto them, the faster and smoother creation will be. The true power of hope is in your heart. If you are struggling to get excited about your hope, then you are probably thinking too small. A real hope will stir your soul and make you excited. You can be the proverbial kid in the candy store and choose whatever you want. Do not put limits on yourself. The bigger your hopes, the greater your joy and excitement, which means that you have more fuel to bring to the creation process.

Use this fuel to create a clear picture in your mind of your hope. Imagine the thing that you desire, such as your new car. Create a picture in your mind of your desired car. What does it look like? Imagine the car in detail—its make and model, its color and interior. Imagine yourself inside the car, driving to your favorite place. Put as much detail in your mental picture as possible. Involve all of your senses of sight, sound, touch, taste, and smell. What does your new car smell like? What does it look like? What does it feel like? Spend some time getting really clear about what you desire and putting as much detail into that picture as possible. In Lacey's story about her red dress in chapter 1, she even prayed and asked God to help her get a better picture of what her perfect dress would look like. Cultivating that clear picture facilitated the creation process for her. This mental picture of your hope is also part of spiritual creation.

Your mental picture and your emotions will work together in this process. The more detail you use to picture your hope and the more you imagine yourself receiving it, the easier it will be for you to generate the emotions of receiving that hope. The more excited and joyful you are about your hope, the more your mind and heart will return to add more details to your mental picture. This clear mental picture and your strong emotions about your hope will then energize the creation process.

## The Problem of Expectations and Attachment

Expectations and attachment are impediments to hope. Expectations are limitations that you place upon your hopes. Most expectations pertain to when and how your hope will show up in your life. Your expectations are another way that you try to control the outcome of the

creation process. For example, your hope might be receiving that new car. You may believe that you are going to get that car by saving your money and then buying it from a dealership. You target saving a specific amount, and you feel frustrated when other urgent situations require some of the money you have saved for your car. However, maybe God's plan to bring you that car is completely different. Perhaps your uncle in another state has that car and has decided to purchase a new one. On a whim, your uncle calls you up and offers to sell you the car at a heavily discounted price. In this example, you received the car that you desired, but it did not come to you in the way you expected or in the timing that you expected. Your expectations led you to take certain actions rather than trusting God with the process. Expectations will make it difficult for you to use faith in the creation process, a subject we will discuss in more detail in the next chapter.

It is natural to place expectations upon your hope when you feel emotionally attached to a specific outcome. Attachment is a strong emotional bond to your hope. When you are attached to your hope, you are afraid to let it go because you believe that outcome is the only one that can make you happy. Emotional attachment makes it difficult for you to give up control of the creation process and to allow God to take over. It is a form of desperation. You are so afraid that you will not receive your hope that you try to control the process. You do not fully trust God to bring it to you. Think again about being a child on Christmas Day. You might have had an experience one Christmas when there was one specific gift that you really wanted. It might have been some special new toy that the other kids had—and you wanted one too. When you woke

up Christmas morning, you opened all of your presents with eager anticipation, but you did not get that specific toy. No matter what other wonderful gifts you received or how many gifts you received, you felt disappointed because you did not get the one toy that you wanted when you wanted it. You believed that you could not be happy on Christmas morning without that gift, and your attachment to that one specific outcome spoiled the beauty and joy of what you did receive.

Expectations laden with emotional attachment will slow down or derail your creation process. In order for the creation process to work, you must let go of your specific expectations about how and when your hope will show up in your life. You must also give up your emotional attachment to your hope. You must choose to be okay with not having control over the process, the timing, or even the end result itself. True hope is an assurance in your heart that whatever arrives (and whenever and however it arrives) will be the best thing for you and will be more wonderful than what you have imagined. Then, when your hope does arrive in your life, you will think, "This is better than what I had hoped for!" God can only deliver that kind of outcome to you when you surrender control of the process to Him. You must let go of any expectations about the creation process and allow it to unfold in God's way and timing. The more you surrender, the faster God can work in your life.

Surrendering your expectations and your attachment to your hope does not mean that you cannot hope at all. God desires that you use your agency by hoping—by choosing what you desire to have or experience in this life. Hope is telling God what you desire and where you

want to go in life; it is not plotting out the route to get there. As an example, imagine that you and God are going on a road trip together. You are packed and ready to get into the car, and you move to get into the passenger seat. God says to you "No, you are the one driving. This is your life." So you sit in the driver's seat instead while God gets into the passenger seat. You turn to God to ask where you are going, and He says, "I am not choosing the destination. I want you to choose where you want to go." You reply, "Let's go to Disneyland." God says, "Wonderful. That will be so much fun." God then identifies the most efficient route to your destination. You think you know the best way to get there, so when God tells you to take a certain road, you rebel and say, "That isn't the fastest way to Disneyland." God's planned route did not fit your expectations. At this point, you have a choice. You can choose the route that you expected God to tell you to take. After all, you are the driver. However, if you surrender the route to God, He will get you to the place that you desire. God might take you through another state to pick up a friend on the way or take you on a scenic path so that your journey will be more enjoyable. God might stop at a mall to buy some new clothes to wear on your adventure or stop to visit your mother. No matter the course you take, God will get you to where you desired to be. Not only that, but the outcome will be better than you anticipated because you arrive relaxed in your new clothes with a fun friend to hang out with. The day you visit the park, there is perfect weather and minimal crowds. Had you arrived earlier or later, you would not have gotten the Disneyland experience that you desired. God always desires that you choose your destination. He will never interfere with your

agency, so you will always be the driver. God only asks that you surrender your expectations and attachment so that your journey will be more joyful. Had you held on to your expectations, you might have been frustrated and unhappy at all of the unexpected stops on your road trip rather than just enjoying the journey and trusting that you would receive the best possible outcome.

If God made all of your choices for you and told you what to hope for, then you will never be able to produce enough strong emotion to help the creation process. You will never be more excited about someone else's desire for you than you are about your own desires. The hope must come straight from your heart so that you can truly be joyful and excited about it and truly invested in creating it. When we described hope in the creation process, we discussed feeling your emotions about your hope before developing your mental picture of it. This will help you to avoid attachment. Your joy, gratitude, and love for your hope are not dependent upon it taking a specific form or coming in a certain way. Those emotions developed independently of your mental picture of what that hope looks like in your life. When it comes to creation, the heart must guide the mind, not the other way around. Remember, the feelings of happiness at receiving your hope are an invitation for charity—the fuel for the creation process. If you are attached to your hope and cannot be happy until you have it, then you will constantly be pulled out of balance along the way and not have enough charity to fuel the creation of that hope. It would be like trying to drive a car with no gas. So, get excited about your hope, but let go of any expectations for how it will arrive and any attachment you have to the final outcome.

## Surrender Your Hope

Part of releasing your expectations and attachment is surrendering your hope itself to God. You can surrender your hope to God in a manner similar to the repentance process in chapter 5. Pray to God and tell Him that you desire to surrender your hope. Then visualize yourself handing it over to God. Similar to the visualization exercise for the repentance process, watch God receive your hope and then present you with some other gift. Choose to receive that gift and bring it into yourself. Stay mindful through the process and remember to breathe deeply. Keep yourself present in the visualization until you feel complete. If you feel any resistance to surrendering your hope, you can repent of that resistance and forgive yourself. Remember, repentance is surrendering.

There might come a point in your journey when God will ask you to completely surrender your hope—to stop wanting and desiring it. You must be willing to give up that last bit of control and attachment, even if it means that you will never receive your hope. If you are continually staying in balance through the process, surrendering that hope will be easy because you feel content even without that hope. You will already be happy and joyful each day, so surrendering your hope will not feel like you are really giving anything up. Ironically, when you do finally surrender your hope, God can bring it into your life.

Ask yourself if you are ready to surrender your hope. Ask yourself if you can be happy without it. As you ponder these questions and go through the process of surrendering your hope, you might see little strings of attachment to your hope that you did not know were there. As you recognize this emotional attachment to your hope, you can

choose to forgive yourself and repent of that attachment. This allows God to further purify you, and it removes anything in your life that might prevent you from receiving your hope.

The prophet Joseph Smith taught this in the *Lectures on Faith*: "Let us here observe, that a religion that does not require the sacrifice of all things never has power sufficient to produce the faith necessary unto life and salvation; for, from the first existence of man, the faith necessary unto the enjoyment of life and salvation never could be obtained without the sacrifice of all earthly things" (p. 69). Joseph Smith is essentially teaching about surrender here. Without surrender, your faith will not grow. When you are still holding on to your hopes or holding on to the process, then you are still trying to force your hopes to happen. You are still doing it on your own. The more you exercise your hope, faith, and charity, the more they will grow in your life and bring you closer to partnership with God.

Your hopes help you get to know God and to develop faith and trust in Him. Your hopes have such a strong pull on you that they can inspire you to help you develop your hope, faith, and charity. God is thrilled because the creation process not only brings you your hope but also brings you closer to Him. As you go through this process, you will cherish your relationship with God more and feel less attachment to your hopes. The whole practice of hope, faith, and charity is giving God more and more of your heart and giving up everything else so that nothing stands between you and Him. When nothing stands between you and God, then nothing stands between you and everything that God has to give you. Hope, faith, and charity help

you to create perfect unity with God. That is the beauty of this process. Hope, faith, and charity draw you to God and make you like Him.

## Lacey's Story About Surrendering Her Hope to Lose Weight

After I had my fourth child, I put on a significant amount of weight. I did not want to have all this excess weight, so I decided to create hope of being thin. I shared my hope with God and then got to work on it. I fasted and prayed. I dieted and exercised. I repeated affirmations. I worked on repenting of and forgiving various beliefs about myself to help me reach this hope. I did so many things, but the weight barely changed at all. After three years of hard work and focusing on this hope, I was completely worn out and very frustrated. I couldn't understand why the process wasn't working for me, especially when I had experienced so much success creating my hopes with God in the past.

I went to God and prayed to know what to do. I shared with Him that things were not going how I expected them to go and that I'd only had a little success. I told God that I was tired, worn out, and angry that it wasn't working. I asked God what to do. His answer surprised and terrified me; God told me that I needed to surrender my hope of losing the weight and being thin. Fear raced into my mind. If I surrender this hope, what will prevent me from gaining even more weight and getting even bigger? As I felt my fear in response to God's answer, I realized something very important. I realized that I had not formed my hope in the right way. Instead of creating my hope with joy, I was using fear to fuel my creation process and that was preventing me from creating effectively with God. I was *afraid* of not receiving my hope. I realized that I had an unhealthy obsession about my weight. I was afraid of it and kept judging myself and my body as bad. I was attached to my hope, meaning that I couldn't be happy without it. That attachment and fear were derailing the creation process.

I spent the next several weeks working through my unhealthy beliefs about my weight. I spent a lot of time crying and forgiving myself for my beliefs. I forgave my body for carrying the extra weight. I would visualize myself carrying even more excess weight and would send love to myself as that person. I worked to love myself and my body at my current weight just as much as I would if I were thinner. I used this process to help me to let go of my attachment to my hope of being thin. I knew that it could only come into my life if I surrendered the hope itself and let go of my attachment. I needed to be happy as I was in order to receive this hope from God.

This was an important hope for me with a lot of accompanying emotional baggage, so it took me some time to work through everything and get to a place of peace and charity related to this hope. I felt so much gratitude to God for asking me to surrender this hope and my attachment to it so that I could see what was holding me back. Before that moment, I didn't fully comprehend all of the heaviness and fear associated with that hope. As I worked on repentance and forgiveness to release my attachment to that hope, my balance with God became even stronger. I felt a renewed sense of peace and joy regarding all of my hopes, including this one. It paid off. Over the next year, I started to lose weight. It was not quick, but that

didn't bother me because I was in balance with God and felt peace and happiness no matter what my weight was.

## Hope Is a Gift From God

Hope, faith, and charity are gifts from God. When you feel doubt or fear about whether you can receive your hope, pray that God will brighten your hope and remove your fear. The "Comforter filleth with hope and perfect love" (Moroni 8:26). Through the Holy Ghost, God delivers greater hope to you. Involve God in every step of the process. God can help you to choose your hope, develop strong love and joy for your hope, and put more details into your mental picture. Give yourself permission to desire your hope. Activate your agency around that hope by choosing it and choosing to use this process to partner with God to create your hope.

Avoid judging your hope as you develop it. In particular, avoid judging your hope as something insignificant or selfish. If you label your hope as something selfish, then you are disrupting the creation process from the outset. The only truly "unworthy" hope would be a hope to cause harm to another person. God honors those things that you desire for yourself. God will not judge your hopes as insignificant or selfish. He merely desires to help you learn to create and to have joy in the process. Repent of any judgments that you have of your hopes from the outset. As you do so, God will give you a clearer picture of what you truly hope for.

You also do not need to worry about your motives for creating a hope. You do not need to worry about whether you motives are "pure" enough. Suppose in the new car example above, your hope for a new car is because you want to look good to the other people in your life.

This means that you have some attachment to this hope. You need that new car in order to feel a certain way—to feel good about yourself. Through the creation process, God will help you to see your attachments so that you can repent of them. Chapter 9 will discuss this in more detail. If you recognize that attachment from the outset, it is even better. You can start repenting of it right way. For now, just allow yourself to hope without judging your hope or judging yourself for desiring that hope. Just go with something that you believe will bring you joy. Trust that God will help you to see any attachments, or impure motives, that you might be pinning on your hopes.

Through the whole process of creating your hope, strive to stay in balance with God. Embrace the emotions like excitement, love, joy, and gratitude that accompany your hope. Fear and doubt will likely creep into your mind many times in this process. At times, you might feel unworthy or undeserving of your beautiful hope. You might wonder if God wants to give this hope to you. You might start worrying about all of the obstacles standing between you and your hope. Doubt and fear are part of the process. Do not be afraid of them, and do not judge yourself for experiencing them. Even the doubt and fear can be a gift to you because they show you the beliefs in your life that are preventing you from creating your hope. They show you your expectations and attachments. Repent of those doubts and fears, and ask Jesus Christ to purify them for you and turn them into confidence-building, empowering beliefs. Remember that hope is a gift from God! Continue to pray for that hope.

One way that God seeks to brighten your hope is through the experiences that show up in your life. As you

go through the creation process, people who have what you desire will show up in your life. This is evidence that you are on the right path and that your hope is starting to manifest in the physical world. However, the way you respond to those experiences can either accelerate the arrival of your hope or block it. As an example, suppose you have always wanted to have a child, but you have not been able to get pregnant. You create a glorious hope around having a baby. Then you get a call from a friend who tells you that she is pregnant. You express your happiness for her, but after you get off the phone, you are hit with sorrow, pain, and jealousy. You wonder why it is so easy for everyone else to get pregnant. You wonder if God does not trust you with a baby or if you just are not good enough to receive that blessing. You might even feel that your friend does not deserve to get pregnant again because she has three children already. This type of response pulls you out of balance with God and blocks you from receiving your hope.

The purpose of this experience with your friend is to help you brighten your hope. God's intention is to help you to see the limiting beliefs about yourself that are preventing that hope from coming into your life. For example, when you received that call from your friend, you might have felt that you do not deserve to have a baby or that God does not trust you. These are limiting beliefs; they do not represent God's truth about you. This experience was designed to show you those beliefs so that you can repent of them and allow God to give you true, empowering beliefs. This will get you back into balance with God and get the creation process back on track. The danger is that you might allow yourself to get stuck in the sorrow,

pain, and jealousy of this experience, which will keep you out of balance with God and limit the creation process.

Now suppose that on a different day, you are walking in the park and you see a young mother holding an infant. You recognize that this is a gift from God to strengthen and brighten your hope. You tell God: "Yes, this is what I want!" You notice how tender the mother is with her infant, and you imagine yourself with your own baby. You allow yourself to feel the love and gratitude for your own future baby. If any doubt, fear, or jealousy come up, you repent of them in that moment and pray to be restored to balance. Seeing the mother and baby was a gift to you from God, and it is a sign that you are on the right path. They are appearing in your life to help you break any barriers that may have prevented you from receiving your hope in the past. Receive that gift with gratitude and joy.

In any situation or circumstance in your life, you can choose whether that situation will bring you closer to what you desire or further away from what you desire. You choose your response to those situations and circumstances and whether you stay in balance with God. You choose whether you are willing to look inside yourself to discover what beliefs are keeping you out of balance. You can also choose to repent of those beliefs. We encourage you to choose the desires of your heart. Choose to use everything that shows up in your life as more power in the creation process. Choose to stay in balance with God. Remember that you can always ask God to bless you with stronger hope.

## Lacey's Story About Creating a Hope for a Home

As I was learning from God about using hope, faith, and charity as a framework for creation, I felt a desire to test these principles on a big hope. My husband and I had often talked about building a home, but it had always felt like something that was far in the future. I loved where we were currently living, but I started to feel like it was time for us to move. The desire to move grew, and I decided to work on developing a hope for a home.

I wasn't sure yet what I wanted my new home to look like, so I allowed myself to start dreaming about it. In the evening after my children went to bed, my husband and I would watch a show together. As we watched, I would pull out graph paper, a ruler, and a pencil and start drawing floor plans. I continued to work on my plans during the day when I had free time. I would imagine myself living in each of the different floorplans—cooking in the kitchen, going upstairs to put laundry away, etc. I let myself get lost in my imagination and had fun envisioning a new home.

When I visited friends' and family members' homes, I would notice the layouts and features of that home. If there were a particular space that I liked, I would ask them to give me a tape measure so that I could record the room's dimensions and add it to my drawings. I loved looking at homes and allowed myself to really enjoy the process. I kept praying about this hope to build my home, but I didn't feel rushed in the process. I loved where we were living, so I was perfectly happy without receiving this hope. I just continued to create the hope with as much detail as I wanted and let God know what my hope was. I loved telling Him about the details that I desired for my

home. I let God know that someday I wanted to have this home and that I was grateful for the peace I felt about it.

After a couple months of creating my hope, I felt a desire to look at properties. My sister had recently moved to a city with cheaper vacant lots compared to nearby areas, so I thought it would be fun to look at them. I invited my husband to go with me. He knew that I had been working on creating this hope and that I was excited about it, so he willingly went with me. We found a couple lots that we thought would work for our family. I took pictures of those lots and wrote down the phone numbers.

A few days later, I felt that I wanted to call about those lots we had looked at. This would typically be a chore that I would leave to my husband, so it surprised me that I felt like calling myself to make my inquiries. I remained balanced and peaceful, even while feeling a great desire to call. The call went great. The lot we wanted was selling at a great price, and we could bring our own builder. It was ready for us to buy. When my husband got home from work, I told him the news. He immediately felt peaceful about the idea of buying this lot. Both of us felt like it was time to move forward on building our own home. It felt so joyful—not stressful at all. I knew that none of it would have happened had I not allowed myself to dream and create a hope with God.

Hope is an incredibly powerful tool in your creation tool kit. Hope allows you to feel the emotions of receiving

what you desire and paint a strong mental picture of that desire. After you have done this, you must choose to create your hope so that your agency can activate spiritual creation. Your excitement and enthusiasm for receiving your cherished desires will bolster the creation process and help keep you in balance. Part of hope is also letting go of any expectations for how and when that hope might arrive in your life and releasing any emotional attachment to a specific outcome. God will help sustain your hope and keep it bright as you go through this process. Faith is the vehicle that gets you to your hopes.

# Chapter 9
## Faith

Faith is the second element of the creation process. It encompasses the work that you need to do to receive what you desire. Faith is not about laboring and forcing your hope into existence or controlling the process. It is about taking the right actions—those that keep you grounded in God's power and your power. Faith is what you do to truly maximize God's power in your life.

## What Is Faith?

The scriptures indicate that "faith is not to have a perfect knowledge of things; therefore if you have faith ye hope for things which are not seen, which are true" (Alma 32:21). Essentially, the scriptures teach that faith is something that almost defies logic. It is a firmly rooted belief in something even when there is no evidence for it. Trust and belief are like the little sisters of faith, which is stronger, purer, and more powerful than just trusting or believing. It takes faith to activate your agency to create what you desire. While there are many things that you can do to strengthen your faith, it is ultimately a gift from God, just

like hope and charity. God helps you on your journey by blessing you with greater faith. At any time on your creation journey, you can pray to God and ask for more faith.

## Faith in the Creation Process

Faith is the journey you take to receive your hope from God. Faith must undergird all of your actions in the process. Your true self naturally trusts God and believes that you can create your hope with Him. The trick is choosing to allow your true self to govern what you do through the process, what you think about the process, and how you feel about the process. Faith is not about hard work. It is about doing the work to let your spiritual nature guide your thoughts, emotions, and actions about your hope and the creation process. As such, there are three main areas of faith—faith as belief, faith as confidence, and faith as action.

### Faith as Belief

Belief is in your mind. Beliefs are thoughts that you think repeatedly, both conscious and unconscious. You started the creation process by developing a visualization of your hope in your mind. But what often happens is that instead of holding on to that beautiful thought, you let your mind slip into worries, doubts, and fears that you will not receive what you desire. You might feel afraid that God will not pull through for you because of experiences you have had in the past. You might worry that you are not doing enough. You might question whether your desire is even something that is possible. These thoughts and beliefs are not in alignment with what you desire, nor are they evidence of faith. Faith as belief means recognizing when you fall into a thought pattern that is not

congruent with receiving your hope and changing that pattern through repentance. Then God will give you new beliefs that are supportive of your creation.

A good way to start your faith journey is to assess your level of faith in three areas: (1) your faith in God, (2) your faith in yourself, and (3) your faith in your hope. Suppose you have the hope of finding the perfect new home. You write out the details of what you desire in your home—how it looks, how many rooms it has, what it looks like, and where it is located. You can see in your mind what the house and property look like. You surrender that hope to God and ask God to co-create your perfect house with you. You are now standing at the beginning of the creation process. At this point, you can assess your level of faith about your creation.

Ask yourself the following questions and rate yourself on a scale from 1 to 10, with 1 representing no belief and 10 representing perfect belief:

- How much do I believe that God can provide me with this hope?

- How much do I believe that I can stay balanced with God and am worthy enough to receive this hope?

- How much do I believe that this hope is even possible?

We recommend that you write down your scores on each of these questions, so you can revisit them later in the process to see how your faith in each of these three areas has grown.

It is likely that you did not score a perfect 10 on each of these questions. Returning to the perfect home example,

let's say you rate yourself as a 9 for your belief in God, a 4 for your belief in yourself, and a 6 for your belief that your perfect home is out there. If any of these scores are low, it does not mean that God does not want you to have that hope. It just means that there are some underlying beliefs and emotions that need to be surrendered in order for you to receive that hope.

So, what do you do if your faith scores are not perfect? First, you can repent of those scores. Follow the steps outlined in chapter 5 and repent of each of these low scores. Repentance is necessary because you will need God's help to change your thoughts and deep-rooted beliefs. You can also be more mindful of your thoughts throughout the day. You have power over your mind; you can direct your thoughts. When you find your mind bringing up doubt, acknowledge those thoughts, thank them for showing up to teach you, and then release them. Then you can choose a more supportive thought about receiving your hope. Do the work necessary to train your mind to believe in your hope. If it helps, you can repeat affirmations or spend some time in meditation to quiet your mind. Staying in balance with God will also help keep your mind on an empowering track.

At any time during the creation process, you can check in with yourself and reassess your faith scores in these three areas. Over time, your scores will grow, especially as you seek to stay balanced and choose positive thoughts and beliefs about your hopes. Your faith scores are a simple tool that you can use to be more in tune with your beliefs. You will then feel empowered to repent of limiting beliefs and to choose new beliefs.

### *Faith as Confidence*

Faith as confidence is about your emotions. Faith is staying in the emotions (joy, peace, love, gratitude) of receiving your hope from God. Your faith will grow stronger the more you stay balanced, so if you desire to *feel* confident about the creation process then you need to focus on being partnered with God through staying in balance. Remember, your emotions help you to stay in charity, which is the primary fuel for creation. You must be mindful that you are cultivating and staying in the emotions of your hope rather than the emotions of your current circumstances. It is easy to get pulled out of balance when you dwell on what you do not like about your life.

We will return again to the perfect home example. Suppose that one morning you spent ten minutes in quiet meditation just visualizing your perfect home. You saw each room and how beautifully decorated it was. You saw your family living comfortably and happily in this home. You imagined all the details of this home. As you did so, you cultivated the feelings of living in this home. You felt so much gratitude for this perfect home. You felt excited about the prospect of moving into it. You felt happy about being in this new home. By the time your meditation was done, you were buoyant and joyful after reviewing this spiritual creation in your mind. The challenge is to hang onto those emotions throughout the day.

Now suppose you really do not like the house you are living in now. It might be too small. Maybe it is a poorly maintained rental. You might not like the layout. It could be drafty or have electrical and plumbing problems. Maybe you go into your kitchen to cook something, and you are aggravated that you have so little space to work in.

Pay attention to your emotions and thoughts about your current home throughout the day. Those feelings of frustration, annoyance, and anger at your current house will push out the joy and excitement of living in your perfect home in the future. The creation process will be faster and more efficient if you can go through the day living with the emotions of what you desire rather than the emotions of what you do not desire. As you cook in your small kitchen with no space to work, let your heart be excited about the day when you will be cooking in your perfect kitchen. Stay in the emotion of what you desire as often as you can.

Whenever you find yourself slipping out the emotions of receiving your hope, that is a signal to you that you need to get back into balance. Pray that God will get you back into balance and strengthen your faith. Repent of any emotions or thoughts that you do not want. Then take a few minutes to close your eyes, put your hands on your heart, and visualize what you desire. As you visualize it, feel the emotion of receiving your beautiful hope. It is not enough to just see it—you must *feel* it. Recapture that emotion and then return to your daily activities.

While living in the emotions of what you desire is a great way to bring your hope into your life, keep in mind that it is even more powerful to truly honor and love what you currently have. The more you embrace and love your small kitchen and imperfect house, the more you allow new things to flow into your life. Forgive your small kitchen for being what it is *and* forgive yourself for judging your kitchen as "too small." This will unchain you from the small kitchen. Seek to be truly present with the life you have and to love it in all of its imperfections. As a good and wise steward, you infuse everything in your

stewardship with love and care. You treat everything as a gift from God, even when that gift appears to be imperfect on the surface. When you feel perfect love for what you have, you are in your most powerful state of creation. From that state, the imperfections of your life are free to melt away to allow in the hope that you desire. As much as possible, seek to love and accept what is. In the moments when that is difficult, cast your mind to the future day when you receive your hope and live from that joy.

Faith as confidence is a beautiful thing. Allow yourself to live in peace and joy. Reach into that future day when you receive what you desire, harness those emotions, and then pull them into the present moment. Allow yourself to live as if your petition has already been granted. What better way to show God your faith than to feel joy right now? That joy means that you *know* your prayers are being answered, and you are confident that you will receive your hope. You have taken your focus off your doubts and are keeping your focus on what you desire.

### *Faith as Action*

Faith is more than just belief and confidence because it requires you to exercise your agency and put forth some work. "Even so faith, if it hath not works, is dead, being alone" (James 2:17). However, *the work of faith is not what you think it is!* It is not what your cultural programming has conditioned you to believe. Most people believe that they need to work hard in order to receive something. Most people feel that if they do not put forth 100 percent effort then God will not deem them worthy of receiving what they desire. However, the work of faith is not about exerting all of your effort or exhausting yourself to get

**149**

something. It is about having enough trust in God to step back and let Him do most of the work.

Your job is to work *appropriately* in a way that maximizes your personal power and God's power in your life. In chapter 3, we discussed how your power is greatest when you are centered and balanced with God in the present moment. Then you have full access to God's power and you are standing in your most powerful state. The work of faith is about doing whatever it takes to stay in that place of power. This means that the primary work of faith is staying in balance. The secondary work of faith is taking inspired action. God does expect you to take some action to help create your hope, but it is only what you are inspired to do rather than an effort to force or control the process or make the creation happen on your own. When you are in balance, you will more easily discern what those actions are.

### *The Work of Staying in Balance—Repentance and Forgiveness*

The most important thing that you can do to create your hope is to stay balanced with God. This allows God's power to be fully active in your life. You must continually stay aware of your mental, emotional, and physical state and make choices that will get you back into balance after you have fallen out of it. We have discussed how you can pray and ask for a reset or do a longer visualization to get you back into balance (see chapter 4). We have also discussed that you can repent of and forgive any thoughts, emotions, or experiences that are not in alignment with your hopes and that pull you out of balance (see chapters 5 and 6).

Repentance and forgiveness are two of the most effective things you can do to help yourself stay in balance. *Repentance and forgiveness are your primary work in the creation process.* As you are waiting for God to bring your hope to you, you will have experiences that will bring up your emotional baggage, which includes limiting beliefs, past painful experiences, and other things that distress you. Your primary work on this journey is to notice when those things come up and to repent of them by giving them to Jesus Christ to be changed and purified. Forgiving these experiences, yourself, and others also helps to change your mental and emotional outlook and to heal past trauma. Most of the work you will do in the creation process is using repentance and forgiveness to heal anything in your life that is pulling you out of balance and that is inconsistent with receiving your hope.

Our perfect home example illustrates this. Maybe you are doing a great job at staying in the emotions of your perfect home throughout the day but whenever you use your debit card you start to worry that you will not be able to afford your perfect home. You notice when it happens and get back into balance, but you feel a little frustrated that it happens every single time you spend any money. You can repent of this pattern, meaning you can surrender it to Jesus Christ for purification. Jesus Christ can help you to get unstuck from this pattern and to change it to a new pattern. God does not intend for you to do this on your own; that is why you have been given a Savior. Your most important work is to call upon Jesus Christ to change the emotional and mental patterns in your life that you cannot change on your own. Any time in the creation process that you feel any doubt, fear, or discouragement

about the process, repent of those emotions and patterns and allow Christ to heal and change them for you.

### *Embracing Inspired Action and Eschewing Control*

The other component of your work of faith is inspired action. Again, this does not mean making a long to-do list of all of the things that you think you need to do to make your hope happen. It does not mean that you do all of the things that you think you *should* do. You cannot force your hope into existence. All that God expects from you (aside from staying balanced) is take those actions that you are *inspired* to take. Think about that word *inspire*. It means "to spur on; to exert an animating, enlivening, or exalting influence on."[11] Inspired actions will have an enlivening effect on you; they will make you feel excited and drawn forward, rather than being pushed from behind. Inspired actions will be things that you want to do and feel motivated to do. They will not feel like a burden or a chore. Inspired actions resonate with what is in your heart. God will lead you to your hope through the desires of your heart, so it is important to keep your heart open and stay in tune with its desires. Every day, you focus on only putting forth action toward your hope when you feel a desire to do it and when it honors you. If you feel that you *should* do something, it is *not* inspired action. Inspired action will be what you *want* to do. Sometimes you might feel like you are doing nothing toward your hope, and that is okay. The temptation might be to return to your to-do lists because you fear that you will not receive your hope if you are not doing enough. Resist that temptation and

---

[11] https://www.merriam-webster.com/dictionary/inspire

focus on doing what is in your heart. Repent of the belief that you are not doing enough.

Your inspired actions will often seem random and unconnected to your hopes. That is all part of the process. Embrace the randomness of it all. God chooses to use inspired actions that seem random to you so you will know that you are not in control of this process. God will deliver your hope to you in unexpected ways so you will acknowledge Him as the deliverer, through your faith and staying in balance—not through all of your hard work. You must surrender all control. If you revert to plans and to-do lists, then you are taking control of the process and limiting God's power in your life. Give up the lists and instead follow the desires of your heart. You are not trying to perform your way to your hope. Sit back and allow God to do the work.

To illustrate that randomness, I (Lacey) was looking for a notebook that one of my children had misplaced. The notebook had a particularly important list in it and I needed to find it so I could progress in my work for that day. I couldn't find it anywhere. As I was searching my house, I found one of my daughter's hair bows. I didn't want to put it away that moment because I was in the middle of searching for my notebook, so I clipped it into my hair so I would not forget it and continued my search for the notebook. A pair of glasses caught my attention and I had the thought, "I wonder how I would look with these glasses on?" I thought that the combination of those glasses with my daughter's hair bow would be funny, so I had a strong impulse to go to the bathroom to look at myself in the mirror. As I was walking to the bathroom, the thought flashed through my mind that looking for my

notebook was more important than looking at myself in the mirror. But I ignored that thought and went to go look in the mirror anyway. As soon as I went into my bathroom, I saw my notebook on the bathroom counter. I thought to myself, "God, you are too good! You led me to a hair bow and some interesting glasses and nudged me to go look at myself in the mirror—all to find my notebook? You are good!" God led to me my notebook through some random silliness. (And my stylish look did not disappoint!) God uses the unexpected to bring about the best for you.

In The Book of Mormon, Nephi and his brothers were commanded to return to Jerusalem to retrieve a set of brass plates from Laban so their family could take the scriptures into the wilderness with them. After two failed attempts to get the plates, the brothers' emotions were running high. Nephi volunteered to go back on his own to get the plates. He indicated that he "was led by the Spirit, not knowing beforehand the things which I should do" (1 Nephi 4:6). Through a series of miraculous circumstances, Nephi was able to retrieve the brass plates and return to his family. It all worked out for him. He allowed God to do the heavy lifting; he merely followed his heart and watched the miracle play out. It can be the same in your life. You can be led by inspired action without knowing how those things will bring your hope into your life.

In the perfect home example, you might be tempted to make a list of tasks that would help you get your home—get a realtor, look through houses online, go see houses in person. But if you have surrendered this hope to God, you do not proceed by making a list of things you feel you need to do. Instead, you make sure you are balanced with God and then follow the desires of your heart. You might

be driving home from the grocery store and feel like you want to take a different road home. As you drive, you pass the perfect home with a "For Sale" sign in front of it. Or you might feel like you want to call an old friend and go play tennis with him. While you are at the tennis court, your friend introduces you to someone and that person is trying to sell their home—a home that turns out to be perfect for you. These are examples of ways that God will lead and direct you to your perfect home through random circumstances that result from your inspired actions.

It bears repeating that this is what many people struggle the most with—letting go of control. Our society values action, and you have probably been taught from a young age that you will not have what you want unless you work for it. Many people start to be overwhelmed with fear of not receiving what they desire when they are not doing anything active toward their hopes. Their actions are really an attempt to run away from or numb the fear. That fear can undermine the whole process. You must repent of that fear by taking it to Jesus Christ and asking Him to purify it and transform it into love. *The key to creation is less action and more focus on God.* Keep reminding yourself that God does not desire for you to be busy and stressed. Instead, God desires to infuse your life with power. One purpose of this book is to help you to get out of the way so that God can show up more fully for you. Focus on being balanced and following your heart and leave most of the action to God.

## The Trial of Faith

You may have heard the phrase "trial of your faith" as it is used often in the scriptures. As Moroni taught: "I would show unto the world that faith is things which are

hoped for and not seen; wherefore, dispute not because ye see not, for ye receive no witness until after the trial of your faith" (Ether 12:6). Your life might get a little chaotic when you start the creation process. In order for you to repent of the beliefs, emotions, and experiences that are incompatible with your hope, you must first see and acknowledge them so that you can make a conscious choice to surrender them to Jesus Christ. You cannot repent of something that you are unaware of. God will bring experiences into your life to help show you those incompatible thoughts, emotions, and experiences, and some of these experiences might be very triggering to you. Your most cherished hopes often have a lot of past emotional and mental baggage associated with them. God knows that you need to work with Jesus Christ to heal your past so that the creation process will work, and you can draw your hope to you. Therefore, it might feel like your life is falling apart because you are having experiences that bring up this past pain. It might feel that you are getting further from your hope rather than closer to it.

This is normal. It is actually a very good thing because it means that all of this repressed energy is ready to be released so that you can allow something new—your hope—into your life. Understanding what is happening and why it is happening will help you to stay on course in creating your hope. It will help you to stay balanced as your emotional baggage is being processed. When you see the chaos in your life, it does not mean that the process is not working or that God does not want you to have what you desire. It does not mean that you are not good enough or worthy enough to receive your hope. It just means that there is more work for you to do—more repentance

and forgiveness—so that you have the capacity to receive
your hope. In order to receive what you desire, you must
become a person who feels fully worthy and deserving
of that desire. Repentance and forgiveness help you to
become that person. You can choose to hold on to the past
or you can choose to repent and forgive so that you can
create your hope with God.

We will illustrate this principle with an analogy.
Suppose you are standing at the base of a cliff that is sep-
arating you from your hope. You want to get to the top
of the cliff so that you can receive your hope. You get a
running start and try to jump up. But the cliff is just too
big for you to jump on your own, so you end up falling to
the ground and not making it to your destination. You feel
pain and frustration. You might even feel angry at God
because you didn't feel that God helped you. And you still
haven't been able to create your hope. This is illustrated
in Figure 5.

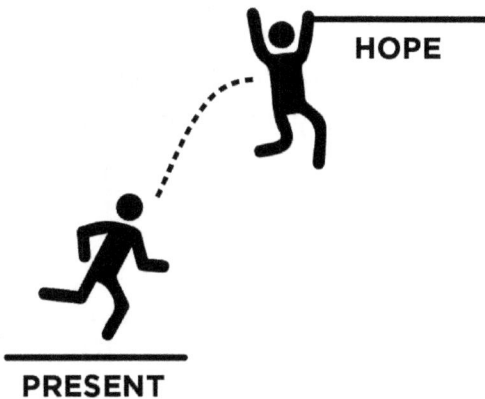

**Figure 5: Trying to Do It on Your Own**

Figure 6 shows the alternative. In Figure 6, you know that you are going to fall after starting to create your hope, meaning that you know that you are going to have some uncomfortable experiences that show you things in your life that need to be healed through forgiveness and repentance. Instead of resisting this fall or trying to get to your hope on your own, you allow the fall to happen. You accept these uncomfortable and challenging situations and trust that they will help you to receive what you desire. When those situations show up, you allow yourself to feel any sorrow, anger, or fear that they bring with them. You forgive all of the people involved, including yourself. You take the situation and surrender it to Jesus Christ through repentance. You allow yourself to receive Jesus' gift back to you and allow yourself to be healed and changed in the process. Accepting these experiences is like stepping off a cliff. You feel that it is taking you further away from your hope. But there is actually a trampoline at the bottom of that cliff. When you step off the cliff, you land on the trampoline and it catapults you across the chasm so that you land on the other side. You receive your hope. By accepting these challenging experiences instead of running away from them, you actually arrive at your hope faster and with less effort.

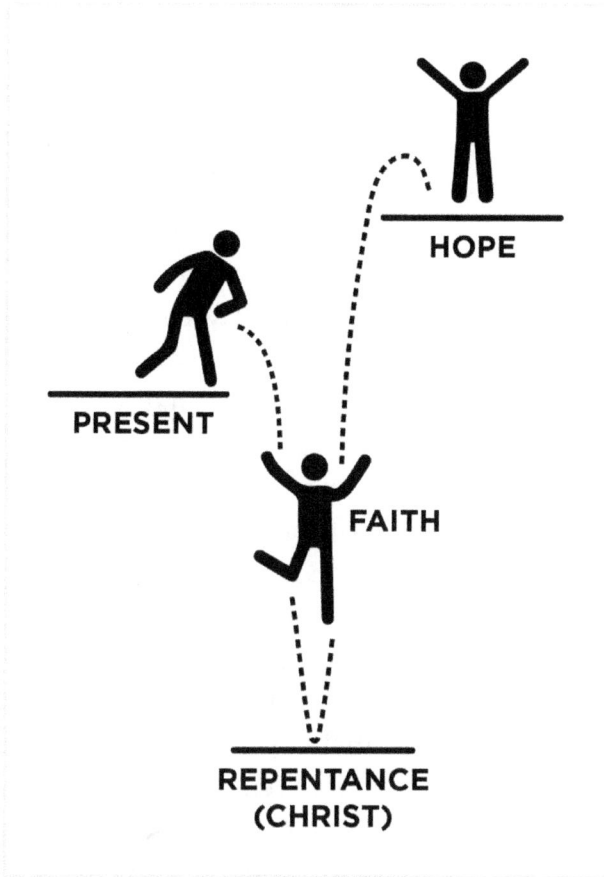

**Figure 6: Using the Trial of Your Faith to Catapult You**

This is the trial of your faith. It is recognizing that when you exercise your faith to try to create your hope, you will have experiences that make your hope feel impossible. You will have experiences that bring up your mental and emotional baggage. You pass the trial when you recognize that those experiences are designed to help you get to your hope faster, and you choose to use them to accelerate your healing.

Many people treat the trial of their faith as a miserable hardship that they suffer through in order to get what they

desire. They believe that the greater the misery they experience, the greater their faith. Perhaps for you this phrase carries a connotation of great suffering through difficult circumstances. However, faith is not meant to be miserable; it is intended to be joyful. The trial of your faith is not about being willing to endure miserable circumstances until God answers your prayer. The trial of your faith is whether you choose to stay balanced throughout the whole creation process so that your current circumstances are as joyful as receiving what you desire. The challenging part of the trial is being aware enough of your emotions and thoughts to notice when you get pulled out of balance, to repent and forgive, and to rebalance yourself and refocus on God. Another challenging part of the trial is giving up control over the process and giving up your need to force your hopes into existence through hard work. The work of receiving your hopes is not intended to be miserable hardship, instead it will be the most joyful work that you will ever do. Repentance and forgiveness will make you feel free. Sometimes the most difficult part of the faith journey to your hope is allowing it to be as easy and effortless as God intends it to be.

Staying balanced might be challenging at first. If you get overwhelmed or discouraged by the process, then you are out of balance. Keep using the tools and strategies in this book—repentance, forgiveness, and the visualization from chapter 4—to help get yourself back into balance. It is okay if your faith is not perfect at the beginning. That will not prevent you from receiving your hope. In the New Testament, there is a beautiful story of a man who brought his son to Jesus to be healed. The son had been possessed by evil spirits since he was a child, and he was a danger

to himself and others. "Jesus said unto him, If thou canst believe, all things are possible to him that believeth. And straightway the father of the child cried out, and said with tears, Lord, I believe; help thou mine unbelief" (Mark 9:23–24). The father's plea is so beautiful because it shows his vulnerability as a human being.

As you apply this story to your own life, you can look at unbelief in two ways. The most common form is to not believe enough, but the other form is to believe in things that are not true. Believing that you are unworthy of God's help or blessings is a lack of faith because that statement does not represent God's truth about you. You do not need to earn your hopes through any particular actions; they are given to you by God because He loves you and desires to bless you. God's truth about you is that you are worthy to receive what you desire. Many people believe enough to approach God and to petition Him for help, but they do not always have the faith to receive God's help because of some limiting belief or past pattern. In your petitions, you can simultaneously beg God to give you your hope *and* to give you the faith that you lack. God will joyfully do so. He will also help your unbelief by showing you the patterns and beliefs that are not in harmony with God's truth. Your faith is something that you can surrender to God for purification. As you walk on this journey of faith, God will help your faith to grow as you repent and let go of control. "For by grace are ye saved through faith; and that not of yourselves: it is the gift of God" (Ephesians 2:8). Faith itself is a beautiful gift from God and you can receive that gift as you walk the path of faith, repent continually, follow your heart, and stay balanced with God.

Recognize that on your faith journey, there will still be ups and downs. There will be times when you feel some heavy emotions coming up or when you get triggered. You can navigate those emotions—grief, fear, anger, sorrow, shame—and still stay in balance. Ask God to help you feel and express those emotions as they arise. If you are balanced, they will surface and pass quickly. When they pass, you will be restored to peace, love, and joy. That is natural and normal. However, if you let those heavy emotions pull you out of balance, they will linger and get stuck. Stay in balance with God and ask Him to help you to navigate any emotions that arise.

When you start on the path of creation, every experience that comes into your life is designed to bring that hope to you in the most efficient way possible. The more conscious you are of the beliefs and emotions those experiences bring up, the more you will see what needs to be healed through repentance and forgiveness. God is guiding you through the whole process. The most important work you will do to receive your hope is to stay aware of your emotions and thoughts and to repent every single day. The more you do this, the easier it will be to stay in balance and to hold on to the emotions of the beautiful things that you desire.

## Lacey's Story About Using Faith to Build Her Home

After my husband and I bought the lot for our home, I knew that the next step was to engage an architect. I found a reasonably priced architect and took my drawings to him. He got to work on drawing the blueprints for our home, and my husband and I met with him often. My husband wanted us to be cautious and not overextend

ourselves financially on the project. When our first esti-
mate of the total home cost came in, he felt stressed about
the costs. He told me that we would need to shrink the
square footage for the home somewhere. The easiest thing
to cut was the upstairs loft. The problem was that I was
so excited about that portion of the house, and it made
me really sad to lose it. The whole time I was creating this
hope, I imagined our new home having the upstairs loft.
I loved that portion of the house plans. But I didn't want
my husband to feel stressed about the home, so I agreed
to cut it.

When we got home from that meeting, I found a quiet
place to go pray. I felt completely devastated. I knew that
it was just an upstairs loft and that we would still be
getting a really great home, but I felt so much sadness
about letting it go. As I prayed, God asked me, "Lacey, do
you want to have your upstairs loft?" I burst into tears and
replied "Yes!" I explained to God all of the reasons why I
wanted it and how much joy it had brought me when I was
creating it. God said, "If that is what you desire, then have
faith and keep your upstairs. I have you and your home."
Peace flooded over me. The feeling was so real and powerful that it almost felt tangible. I knew that somehow it
would work out for me to keep the upstairs portion of the
home. I didn't know how we were going to afford it, but I
felt peace about moving forward.

I talked to my husband, Matt, about my prayer and the
answer I received from God. He responded positively. We
decided to move forward with faith in God and faith in our
hope. We decided to trust that God would bring our hope
to us. The process was not always smooth, and sometimes
we would feel stress and anxiety about the home. But

whenever we felt that we had been pulled out of balance, we would work to get back into balance. If we felt irritated with our contractor, we would repent of those feelings and forgive them. If we felt stressed about money, we would repent of those feelings and forgive ourselves for falling out of balance. When delays came up, we reminded ourselves that God's timing is perfect. We worked to stay joyful and in balance through consistent repentance.

We experienced countless miracles the year that our home was being built. Our hope was getting closer every single day. As the time drew near to close on our new home, a head hunter reached out to Matt about a job prospect. Matt didn't usually explore options like this, but it felt different this time. He felt that he wanted to respond to the head hunter and discuss the job option with him. Within a week of that conversation, Matt interviewed for and was offered a new job. Not only did this job come with a bigger salary—one that would enable us to easily make the new mortgage payment on this bigger home, but other aspects of the job were hopes that Matt had been creating for his own career. God delivered Matt's created hopes to him at the same time that He took care of the mortgage for our new home. Even now, I still feel emotional when I think about how God delivered this hope to us. God came through on His word. He told me to have faith and to keep my upstairs, even if the cost was greater. It was incredible to me that the same week we closed on the new home, Matt was offered this new, better-paying job. Now I live each day in the miracle home that I created with God.

I feel so happy about creating this hope for a home. While we had to do a lot of physical work to receive this home, it paled in comparison with the work of faith that

we had to do. We did so much repenting and so much forgiving. We actively cultivated love for everyone involved and for our new home. We often returned to God for confirmation that our hope was real and He was leading us to it. We prayed for more faith that we could receive our hope. We worked for this miracle, but most of our work was repentance, forgiveness, and inspired action. We were truly working with God.

To summarize, faith sustains you through the creation process. It informs and directs all of your efforts. Faith reminds you that God will do the heavy lifting for you. Your responsibility is to focus on faith as belief, confidence, and action. You do this by staying balanced and taking only inspired actions. When discussing the sacrifices of the patriarch Abraham, James said "Seest thou how faith wrought with his works, and by works was faith made perfect?" (James 2:22). Your works, meaning your repentance and inspired actions, are meant to strengthen and develop your faith. The more you do this, the easier it will be to let go of trying to control the whole process. Your work in the creation process is not about trying to be obedient or to earn a blessing from God. All that God wants from you is that you step back and allow Him to show up in your life. True faith is always partnered with God.

# Chapter 10
## Charity

Hope and faith do not function without charity. The whole process of creation—from your initial hope to the time you receive that hope from God—must be overseen by charity. Charity creates an environment that allows the creation process to flow and succeed. Creation would not work without charity because it drives the entire process forward. Charity fuels the creation process and allows your creations to manifest in the most efficient, beautiful way possible.

### What Is Charity?

Charity is God's love—a celestial force and power. The power, strength, and depth of God's charity is beyond your imagination. It is beyond any love you have ever felt or experienced. Charity is love in its strongest and purest form. It is love free from judgment. God has the ability to hold and to possess charity continually. Humans do not inherently possess charity. One purpose of mortality is to train your body to be able to receive and hold on to charity, and this process requires some time and effort.

Until you can possess charity constantly within yourself, you abide in God's love, His charity. You do this by receiving charity as a gift from God. God will give you this gift whenever you ask for it and choose to receive it. If you keep doing this repeatedly, eventually your body elevates to the point that it can hold on to charity itself. This is how you become more like God.

The prophet Mormon taught the importance of charity:

*"Wherefore, my beloved brethren, if ye have not charity, ye are nothing, for charity never faileth. Wherefore, cleave unto charity, which is the greatest of all, for all things must fail—but charity is the pure love of Christ, and it endureth forever; and whoso is found possessed of it at the last day, it shall be well with him. Wherefore, my beloved brethren, pray unto the Father with all the energy of heart, that ye may be filled with this love, which he hath bestowed upon all who are true followers of his Son, Jesus Christ; that ye may become the sons of God; that when he shall appear we shall be like him, for we shall see him as he is; that we may have this hope; that we may be purified even as he is pure"* (Moroni 7:46–48).

According to this scripture, charity is the supreme virtue. Mormon points out that you must pray to God and ask Him to bless you with charity because you cannot receive or attain it on your own; charity is a gift from God. Notice also that the end of this scripture indicates that receiving charity helps you to change and become like Christ—to be His son or daughter. The practice of praying

for and receiving charity over and over again transforms your life.

When you are in balance with God, you have charity. As we discussed in chapter 4, when you get out of balance you can pray and ask God to get you back into balance. God restores you to balance by blessing you with charity. Therefore, you bring charity into the creation process by staying in balance with God. Faith is necessary to help you continually have charity in your life because it takes faith to focus on repentance and forgiveness rather than working hard to make your hope happen. That work is what allows God's power to operate fully in your life.

## How Charity Influences the Creation Process

If you want to create a life you love, then you need to have as much charity as possible, meaning that you need to be in balance with God throughout the process. When you have God's charity, then your creations will grow and progress. The whole creation process is faster and smoother. When you are not in balance, you do not have charity, and you start blocking and limiting creation. Charity is essential to creation for several reasons.

The first way that charity affects the creation process is that it fully activates God's power and help in your life. There is a perfect balance between your efforts and God's efforts, as illustrated by the balance scale from chapter 2. When your level of effort is right, then God is able to do all of the heavy lifting. Whenever you have charity and are in balance, you are working with God's power, not just your own. Your limited power is coupled with God's omnipotence. God can bend all elements, including time, to His will and purposes. God can shift the elements for you when you are in balance and have charity. In a state of

partnership with God, you are working within the boundaries of higher laws that supersede the laws of the physical world. Charity gives you access to all of the powers of
heaven. If you really desire to have your hope, then receiving charity from God is crucial.

Another way that charity aids the creation process is
that it has the power to change your being. When you
have charity, your body receives divine nourishment and
healing and begins to restore itself to its perfect state. The
longer you stay balanced and receiving God's charity, the
more your body heals. Your body is then able to receive
more from God, including His power, wisdom, strength,
love, and blessings. Charity exponentially increases your
growth and progress as a human being. You are stronger,
smarter, more energetic, healthier, and more emotionally
stable when you have charity. "Therefore, if any man be in
Christ, he is a new creature: old things are passed away;
behold, all things are become new. And all things are of
God, who hath reconciled us to himself by Jesus Christ..."
(2 Corinthians 5:17–18). This scripture makes it clear that
charity transforms you—body and spirit. You can become
a completely new person. You become the kind of person
who is a magnet for the things that you desire.

Third, when you have charity, you are in godly rest.
You are in a state where you are open and able to receive
from God. Your capacity to receive your hopes from God
is naturally limited by your physical body, especially when
you have been subject to years of cultural programming
that make you believe that receiving from God is difficult.
Charity increases your capacity to receive. Learning to stay
in godly rest is the process by which you develop the spiritual gift of receiving from God. You might do everything

else right, but without godly rest you will not be able to receive your hopes from God. We will discuss the importance of this rest in chapter 11. For now, just know that charity opens you up to receive your hopes from God.

Finally, another way that charity helps the creation process is by putting you in an optimal space to receive and recognize revelation from God. The physical work and effort that you put toward receiving your hopes must be inspired action, not frantic efforts to do anything and everything you can to make your hope a reality. You only need to do the work that God directs you to do. When you are not in balance, you start believing that you need to do more than you really need to do. All of the doubt, stress, and fear you experience when you are out of balance make it difficult for you to perceive God's direction for you. When you stay in balance, you are in a state of clarity and God's direction easily flows into your life. It will be easier for you to recognize it and to trust it. You are less likely to second guess and doubt the promptings that you receive when you are filled with charity.

## Charity Is the Sustaining Power

In chapter 1, we used a match as an analogy for agency. Agency is the match that activates spiritual creation. But just like the flame ignited by a match needs fuel to survive, your creation also needs fuel in order for it to manifest in the physical world. This fuel is charity. Charity is the sustaining power that will draw your creation into the physical world. Charity allows the creation process to thrive.

Fear is the opposite of charity because it prevents love from entering into your life. Fear can be very destructive to the creation process because fear is also a sustaining power, like charity. Fear also has the power to take a spiritual creation and turn it into a physical creation. But fear damages everything in the process. It slows creation down. It can warp your final creation into something you do not desire. Fear can even prevent your hope from coming into your life.

Staying balanced ensures that your creation is being sustained by charity rather than fear. Anytime you feel fear in the creation process, repent of that fear. Repent of any situations or beliefs that cause that fear. Ask God to replace your fear with greater charity. Choose to receive that greater endowment of charity.

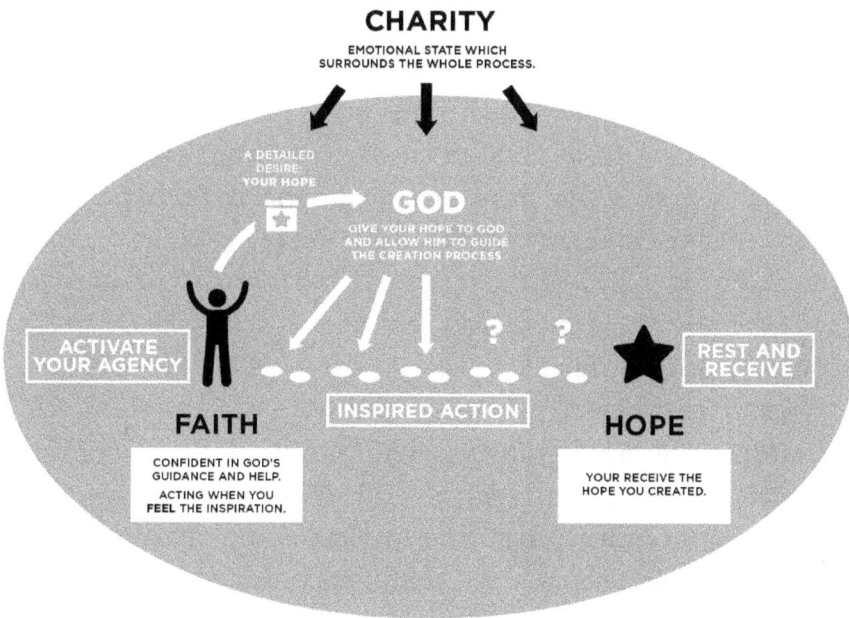

**Figure 7: Charity as the Sustaining Power**

Figure 7 shows how charity acts as the sustaining power for the creation process. You begin by activating your agency and choosing a hope. You then surrender that hope and the whole process over to God. You step forward

in faith by allowing God to direct your actions. Instead of working down a to-do list, you take inspired action. Through the entire process—from creating your hope to taking inspired action to receiving your hope—you are surrounded by and encompassed in charity. As long as you choose to stay in balance, you stay in that environment of charity and let it incubate your hope. Charity sustains both you and your hope until that hope arrives in your life. Charity helps you to rest and open yourself up to receive that hope.

## Lacey's Story About Using Charity to Build Her Home

At one point during the construction of our home, our concrete contractor was getting very difficult to work with. Unbeknownst to us, his business was struggling because he had made some unprofitable financial decisions. He was in the middle of that financial mess when he started working on our home. He would tell us that he needed more money for supplies so that he could get the concrete poured, but would fail to show up after we cut him a check. We started to get really frustrated with the situation. We couldn't fire him because he had already done half of our foundation and had received full payment for the work. If we got another contractor at that point, it would cost us more time and money. The delays on the work meant that we were having to push back other sub-contractors, and the timeline for our new home was getting longer. We often tried to reach out to him, but would receive one excuse after another—an illness in the family or deadlines on other projects. Finally, he confessed that he didn't have the money to finish the project. We figured out that he had taken all of the money we had paid him and used it to

pay off other debts instead of buying the necessary supplies for our home.

This put me and Matt in a very uncomfortable situation, and we were angry. We had been using hope and faith and charity through every stage of this home being built, but we weren't prepared for this obstacle. In our minds, we felt completely justified for our irritation with this contractor, but in my heart, I knew that staying out of charity would limit God's power to make this project work out for our good. I told Matt that we needed to do whatever it took to get back into charity before going any further with this building project.

I started praying and acknowledged that I was hurt and angry. I told God about the whole situation and everything I felt about it. But I also told God that my biggest desire was to stay in charity. I told Him that I wasn't going to stop praying about this until I could fully love this man who had wronged us. As I prayed, more of my pain and emotion came up, and when it did, I would express it, cry about it, and then repent of it and surrender it to Christ. I desired to surrender all of the beliefs and emotions that were preventing me from loving this contractor.

I finally got to a breaking point. I was exhausted and told God I was done. I wanted to be in charity and to feel love for this man, but I was too tired to keep trying. I gave up trying anything and just laid there on my bed. I began to think about this man and his situation. I thought of the fear he must be experiencing, having to support a family and feeling the weight of so much financial debt on his shoulders. I thought about the anxiety he would feel anticipating Matt's or my phone calls, knowing he had done wrong by us. My heart started to ache for him, and I

started to pray for him. I wanted God to ease his burdens so that he could begin to feel God's help and peace again. I knew God would ultimately take care of me and Matt, but I saw that this man was struggling and needed God's help and support too.

I decided that I did not want to add to his misery any longer, so I immediately sent him a text and told him that whatever happened I would choose to respect him as a person. I told him that I was praying for him and couldn't imagine the struggle he must have been going through. I told him I was petitioning God to help him. I concluded my text by saying that I loved him and would not pull that love away because of earthly circumstances.

I knew in that moment that I was back in charity. I could imagine myself in that moment walking right up to this man, giving him a hug, and telling him of my love. It didn't feel weird; it felt real. I felt so relieved to be back in charity and back in balance with God. I surrendered to God the whole situation with the concrete for our home and asked Him to work it out. I felt peace that something good would happen for me and Matt, but also for this contractor.

The next day, I got a phone call from the contractor. He was very humble and came clean to me about the situation with his debts and his poor financial decisions. He said that he was so moved by my text and my compassion towards him that he promised me he was going to do everything he could to make it right and get our home done. He told me he was going to sell a bunch of his tools and equipment to pay for our supplies so that he could make this right. I was apprehensive about him doing something so extreme, but he assured me that he wanted to do this and felt it was

right. I felt peace from God, letting me know that He was working with this man to make His life good as well.

I don't know if the contractor ended up selling everything to get my foundation done, but I know he got it done. And we ended up making up time in other phases of the construction, so it didn't really delay our house project. Working through that challenge really did leave me in a place of great charity for this man. To this day, I still feel love in my heart for him. I have no desire to speak ill of this man or that phase of my home construction. My beautiful experience getting back into charity made it one of my favorite parts of the process.

Charity is the prime incubator for your hopes. When you choose your hope, your agency activates the spiritual creation of your desire. Charity is the sustaining power that will allow that spiritual creation to manifest in the physical world. This is why staying in balance is so important; when you are in balance, your creation is being fueled with the sustaining power of charity—God's power. Charity makes every part of the creation process go more smoothly. Charity also changes *you*. It makes it easier for you to stay in balance and opens you up to the direction that you need throughout the process. Just like the metaphor in chapter 7, charity is the wind driving the whole process forward. Charity can get you to the place that you desire. Your main job is to catch that wind by staying in balance and repenting of anything that pulls you out of balance.

# Chapter 11
## Rest and Receive

Receiving your hopes from God requires some action on your part, such as daily repentance and forgiveness so that you can stay in balance. However, the cycle of creation also includes godly rest. God rested on the seventh day after creating the Earth.[12] He ceased His labors and focused on admiring and loving what He had created. Like God, your use of hope, faith, and charity must also be accompanied by appropriate rest in order for you to receive what you desire. Rest is a critical tool in your creation tool kit—one that is often overlooked and underappreciated. Rest increases your ability to receive.

### Receiving Is a Skill

All of the appropriate effort that you have put toward creating your hopes hinges upon your ability to receive from God. It does not do you any good to create a hope and then not be able to receive it. God invites individuals

---

[12] Genesis 2:2 "And on the seventh day God ended his work which he had made; and he rested on the seventh day from all his work which he had made."

to receive something that He desires to give them. In the scriptures, the word *receive* occurs frequently with mentions of the Holy Ghost, reminding you that the gift is there but that you must choose to receive it. After Jesus was resurrected and appeared to His apostles, He told them to receive the Holy Ghost. "Peace be unto you: as my Father hath sent me, even so send I you. And when he had said this, he breathed on them, and saith unto them, Receive ye the Holy Ghost" (John 20:21–22). Christ's instruction to His apostles was that they needed to choose to receive the Holy Ghost that He desired to bestow upon them. The same is true for other blessings that God desires to give you.

Receiving God's blessings is a skill, which means that it is something you can learn to do and get better at doing. It might feel foreign to refer to receiving as a skill because the idea of receiving seems so easy. It is a very simple thing to choose to receive something. However, even when you choose to receive a gift from God, your capacity to receive it is very limited. Your mortal body can only absorb and process a tiny amount of the love and power that God sends to you. Emotional baggage and limiting beliefs can further hinder your ability to receive. This is why part of the creation process is focused on enhancing your capacity to receive God's blessings.

## The Importance of Rest

So how do you increase your ability to receive from God? Perhaps ironically, the most important thing that you can do to receive more from God is to rest. Resting is synonymous with receiving. Resting is the process of stepping back and allowing your body, mind, and spirit

to rejuvenate. That rejuvenating process elevates you in every way and helps you to stay in balance.

A good analogy for the importance of rest is body building. Body builders spend hours in the gym lifting weights in a series of exercises designed to work each muscle group. The interesting thing is that muscle gain actually happens outside of the gym, not in the weight room. Exercise, such as lifting weights, causes thousands of microscopic tears in the muscle tissue. As the body rests, those tears are healed and knitted together, causing the muscle to grow and creating greater strength. The muscle grows during the rest period! Body builders alternate which muscle groups they are working on so that their muscles have a rest day before being subjected to more stress.

The same is true with your hope, faith, and charity muscles. You go through your daily routine and along the way you are mindful to stay balanced, you repent and forgive often, and you continue to create your hopes and surrender them to God. Through all of these actions, you are exercising your hope, faith, and charity. Your spiritual muscles have been torn, so to speak, and that causes a toll on your physical body. Through resting—particularly rest in God—your hope, faith, and charity will grow.

Remember from chapter 5 that when you repent, you also receive a gift back from Jesus Christ. This gift functions like an upgrade because it is meant to elevate your mind, body, and spirit. When your computer or phone needs a software update, it has to pause all other applications and processes in order to focus on the update. Your device has to "sleep" in order for the upgrade to be completed. When you rest, your mind, body, and spirit are free to be upgraded because they do not have to be focused on

running all of the "applications" in your life, such as your "do the laundry" routine or your "go to work" routine. As you rest, your mind, body, and spirit can all pull in greater strength and power from God.

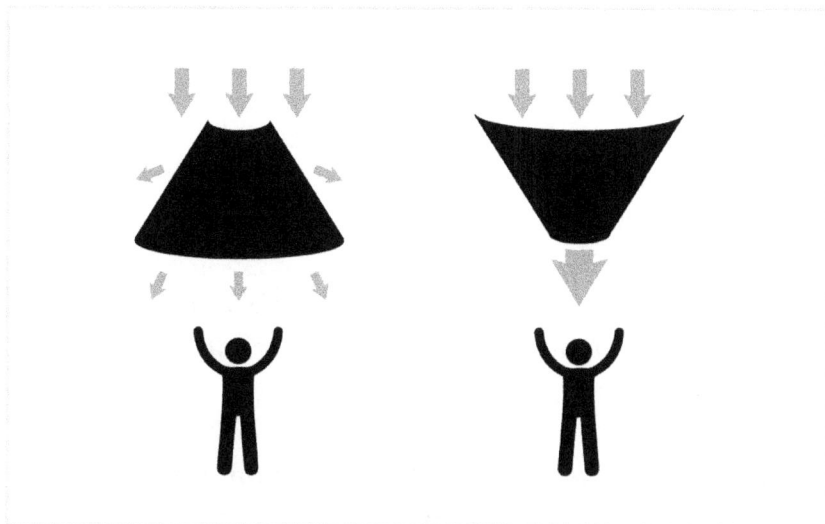

**Figure 8: Funnel of Blessings**

Figure 8 illustrates how this works. Think about a funnel. A funnel is wide at one end to catch the materials that are being poured into it and narrow at the other end to channel those materials into some kind of container. When you are doing everything on your own, your connection to heaven is like a funnel that is turned upside down. The narrow end is pointing toward heaven and receiving only a small amount of what God is sending to you. The wide end is pointing down and scattering everything you receive from heaven into many directions. Your frantic actions to try to catch those blessings cause them to scatter even further. When you choose to rest and to receive from God, you are taking that funnel and flipping it right side up. The wide end now faces toward heaven and can gather

and capture the many blessings that are being showered down upon you. The narrow end keeps those blessings focused on the areas of your hopes and makes it easier for you to receive them. By resting, the funnel can direct your hopes right into your hands. Resting is receiving.

## Resting in God

Resting is more than just ceasing your labors or taking a nap. The kind of rest needed in the creation process is resting in God, which we define as follows:

*Resting in God = a state of stillness where you focus on receiving positive energy (e.g., love, power, etc.) from God*

Certainly, physical rest and relaxation are an important part of stillness. You must pause your labors to have stillness. But it is not enough to just stop doing things. The other part of resting in God is intentionally and consciously receiving nourishment from Him. In fact, God has counseled: "Be still, and know that I am God" (Psalm 46:10). The first thing you must do to rest in God is to be still. When you are in a state of physical stillness, it is easier to align with God and to feel truth, wisdom, strength, and power coming into you. You feel God's presence. The more you intentionally create stillness in your life each day, the more you will be able to keep stillness inside of you through your other activities of the day. It helps you to stay in balance throughout the day.

Your body is like a wave of the sea. You exert physical and spiritual energy as you push forward, just like a wave. However, after the wave exerts its power and rushes up to the seashore, it is pulled back into the ocean to regain

its strength. A wave that exceeds its bounds and moves forward with too much energy is a tsunami, and it leaves destruction in its path. Your body and spirit are the same way. You are intended to expend a certain amount of physical, mental, emotional, and spiritual energy. After that, you need a period of stillness to regain your strength. When you push forward too much and exceed your normal strength, it is destructive to your mind, body, and spirit.

Everyone needs to have rest with God every single day. You must actively create a space in your life where you can be still and focused on receiving love and power from God. Receiving from God might look and feel different each time you do it, but it always involves keeping a focus on God, intentionally choosing to receive from Him, and opening yourself up to receive. One easy way to rest in God is through your breathing. When Adam and Eve were created, they received their breath from God.[13] You also receive your breath from God. When you focus on your breath, you focus on that connection between you and God. You can do this by sitting in a quiet place, putting your hands on your heart, and taking slow, deep breaths. Focus all of your attention on your breathing. As you breathe in, allow yourself to receive love and power from God. It might help to say in your mind, "I am breathing God's love and power into me." Spending a few minutes breathing deeply and focusing on receiving from God is an excellent way to rest in God. If you are uncertain about how to rest in God, start with this breathing exercise.

There are many different ways to rest in God. For example, you might just sit for a few minutes with your hands on your heart feeling God's love pouring into you.

---

[13] "And the Lord God formed man of the dust of the ground, and breathed into his nostrils the breath of life; and man became a living soul." Genesis 2:7

You might sit and enjoy a sunrise or sunset and allow yourself to feel gratitude for the beauty of the earth. You can pray or meditate to invite more stillness into your mind. Listening to certain types of music can invite stillness. You could also just sit with your hands or feet on the grass. You might work on an art project. There is no one prescribed way to rest and receive from God. No matter what you choose to do, the important part is holding the intention to receive strength from God. You might be guided to do something different each time you rest in God. Just be still and let the desires of your heart guide you. As you rest, pray and ask to be balanced with God and ask God to increase your ability to receive. Ask for greater hope, faith, and charity and feel yourself receiving them.

Emotional avoiding behaviors, or numbing, is not resting in God. The difference between rest in God and numbing is your motivation and intention for the activity. Numbing is using some kind of mindless activity, like watching TV or scrolling through social media feeds, to check out from life. You typically do this when you are trying to avoid feeling some kind of unwanted emotion. Numbing is not typically a conscious choice, but rather an impulse to escape. For example, when you have had a difficult day at work, you might come home, sit in front of the TV, and eat potato chips. You are trying to dull your senses so that you do not feel the pain, anger, shame, discouragement or overwhelm that you felt at work that day. The intention and motivation behind a numbing behavior is that you do not feel good emotionally and want to avoid that feeling by checking out. There is nothing inherently wrong with watching TV, and there are times when it can be a beneficial activity. You are numbing when you

spend hours and hours watching TV as a form of escape. The desire to numb your emotions through some activity, like eating food or playing games on your phone, is an indication that you have slipped out of balance without recognizing it. As long as you are numbing, you are out of balance with God. When you feel the urge to numb or check out, it is a good time to stop and quickly assess how you feel. In that moment, you can choose to feel your emotions, surrender them to God, and then get back into balance with Him. Once you are in balance, God can direct you to the activity that your body and soul needs the most, even if it is watching TV and eating potato chips. The difference is that you are resting in God instead of trying to escape your unwanted emotions. You can only rest in God when you are in balance and in tune with the desires of your heart.

While some of your numbing behaviors might be obvious, like watching a lot of TV or scrolling endlessly through your phone, you might engage in other numbing behaviors that seem good, but are really about avoiding your emotions. In order to avoid feeling fearful or unworthy, you might spend an excessive amount of time working and have a hard time setting healthy boundaries on your work life. You might use service—even church service—to numb your emotions. When you feel bad about your life, you might try to avoid that feeling by going out to help other people. You might keep your life so busy that you do not have to stop and feel your own emotions. There is nothing inherently wrong with work or service. In fact, those are valuable activities. The problem is when you use those things to avoid feeling undesirable emotions. If you spend your time avoiding your emotions then you

are not in balance, and you cannot create a life you love from a balance of imbalance. It is crucial to recognize your numbing behaviors so that you can fully feel and acknowledge your emotions. If you do not desire to feel those emotions, then repent of them. Surrender those emotions to Jesus Christ and allow Him to change them. Doing so will put you back into balance.

Many people struggle to get adequate rest. This modern world values action and productiveness, while rest is perceived as an unproductive activity. Many people live in a constant state of stress and overwhelm that keeps them busy every moment of the day. You might feel that you must be busy in order to have the kind of life that you want. However, if you desire to create and to receive your hopes from God, you must learn to rest. When you feel the desire to be still, you need to honor that desire instead of ignoring it because you judge resting as unproductive. The more you honor the desire to rest, the more you will learn to delight in stillness and receiving from God.

Resting is a sign of faith. In order to rest, you must surrender your fear of not getting things done or missing deadlines. You must surrender your fear of not receiving your hope. You have to surrender your fear of what other people will think of you if you take a break instead of doing what you think you are supposed to do. You have to let go of your fear of letting other people down. You might even have to surrender part of your identity and how you view yourself in order to be comfortable and happy resting instead of doing. Resting shows God that you are not trying to do it all on your own, but that you are willing and able to step back and allow Him to do the

work for you. The ability to rest is a good indication that your faith in God is growing.

## How to Know When You Need to Rest in God

In order to have adequate rest in God, you must monitor your needs and desires. If you are in balance and you do not feel a desire to do something, then do not do it. Follow the desires of your heart. It is okay to do what you feel inspired to do and to say no to others when their requests are not aligned with the desires of your heart. When you are in balance, the desires of your heart are also God's desire for you—because when you are in balance, you and God are one. God will invite and entice you to do good—not force or bully you. He entreats rather than commands. That is why He will speak to you through the desires of your heart. When you get to the point that you do not desire to do anything, that is God telling you that you need to rest. If you try to push through that feeling and keep doing and accomplishing things, then you will quickly pull yourself out of balance. The desires of your heart will help you to know when to rest.

An impulse to numb your emotions is also a good sign that you need rest in God. Not only do you use numbing to avoid feeling your emotions, but you might also use numbing behaviors as a misguided attempt to give yourself the rest you know that you need. The problem is that numbing depletes you and might even pull you out of balance because of how you judge your actions. You might think you are resting by watching many hours of TV, but your mind, body, and spirit are craving something else—to rest in God and to receive greater strength. The next time you catch yourself doing a mindless activity and

just checking out, stop and reflect on what you are avoiding. What emotion are you trying to avoid feeling? What situation in your life brought that emotion up for you? In that moment, you can choose to repent and rebalance with God. Pray and ask God what type of rest you need the most in that moment.

When you get out of balance mentally, emotionally, or physically, it could also mean that you need to rest in God in order to be restored. In fact, the more you ignore the impulse to rest, the more unbalanced you will become. Your mind might start to race with worries and concerns about how things will work out. You might struggle to stay fully mentally present with what you are doing. You might experience mood swings or feel stuck in emotions like fear or sorrow. Your body will feel more tired than usual and you might experience food cravings. In general, when you need rest, you will start to feel more vulnerable and easily upset by small things.

Pay close attention to these signs and recognize them as a signal that you need rest. In fact, many of these signs indicate that it has been too long since you rested in God. If you ignore these communications from your mind and body, then the symptoms will get stronger and stronger until you cannot ignore them. You can avoid that by staying aware of how you are doing, noticing whether you are in balance, and noticing what you feel drawn to do. If you are not motivated to do anything or want to check out, then you need to focus on resting with God.

## The Importance of the Sabbath Day

God has blessed you with the Sabbath Day so that you have the time and space in the week to rest. The Sabbath Day is truly a special day. When you honor the sacredness

of the Sabbath, you will be open to the gifts of the Sabbath, including the enhancement of all of your spiritual gifts. Remember that God's work and glory is all about you,[14] so God's day—the Sabbath—is actually all about you too. God has given you the Sabbath so He can return everything possible back to you. You spend the week giving glory to God through your labors. The Sabbath restores to you—in a glorified form—everything you put out during the prior week. It is a day that is specifically set aside for stillness and for you to receive more from God. But you have to choose stillness on that day if you desire to receive God's offering to you. The more you choose to rest in God and receive on the Sabbath, the more you have to give to others and to God in the upcoming week.

The best way to take advantage of the Sabbath is to wake up and intentionally choose to receive from God on that day. Choose to stay balanced with God. Pray and ask God to enhance your ability to receive. Take time on the Sabbath to rest and to cultivate stillness. Engage in activities that help you to feel close to God and that make your heart sing. Follow the desires of your heart. Take the time to talk to God and to draw close to Him. Use the Sabbath to repent and forgive everything that caused you any difficulty during the prior week. When you are intentional about resting and choosing stillness on the Sabbath, then that day will truly be a delight.

## Becky's Story About Learning to Rest

One of the hardest parts of the creation process for me was learning to rest. Resting was so foreign to my way

---

[14] "For behold, this is my work and my glory—to bring to pass the immortality and eternal life of man." Moses 1:39

of living. I had always been an ambitious, driven person. There were things that I wanted from life, and I was willing to work hard to get them. I loved setting goals and working to achieve them—and I had *a lot* of goals. Additionally, I have always been a people pleaser and have always had a strong desire to live up to others' expectations of me. I really wanted people to see me as intelligent, capable, lovable, and righteous. Basically, I wanted everyone to believe that I was perfect.

Because of that, I was always busy working to maintain that illusion of perfection. I remember at one point in my life, I was so very busy. My job was incredibly demanding, partly because I was trying so hard to look like a super star. I was constantly saying yes to more assignments at church and more opportunities to serve. I remember one fall where I would be up until 2 a.m. every night because after I finished my work for the day, I still had to practice the piano so that I could accompany the choir at church for the Christmas concert. I couldn't stomach the idea of letting people down.

The sad thing was that I didn't want to be that busy. I remember one Saturday I came home from helping some other women clean out the apartment of a family that was moving. I came home and sobbed because I was too tired to clean my own home. I started to notice that I would often feel resentment in my heart when I would serve. Yet no matter how tired I was, I would keep dragging myself to different commitments and service opportunities. Anytime a sign-up sheet was passed around at church, I felt that I had to sign up, even if I didn't want to. How else would I maintain this illusion of being perfect? But in my heart, I felt sad and resentful about how much I was giving

and how little was left over for me. I felt burned out and unhappy.

Over time, God showed me that if I wanted to have my hopes, I would need to surrender the identity of "Perfect Becky" over to Him. If I wanted to receive more from God, I needed to start doing less. For me, that meant that I needed to listen more to God. When a sign-up sheet was passed around at church, I had to learn to tune into my heart and listen to it. I could tell when accepting another service assignment would pull me out of balance. In those moments, God would tell me that it was okay to say no and that He would take care of whatever service needed to be given. God told me that He didn't want service to make me unhappy or stressed. He could take care of other people as well, and He could take care of me.

Even with all that, it has taken me awhile to get better at giving myself permission to set a boundary and to say no to something, especially something very good. I have learned to look really closely at my motivations for doing something and ask myself, "Is this what I truly want to do, or I am doing this because I am worried about what other people will think of me if I don't?" I have had to repent of my people-pleasing tendencies many times. I have had to surrender my identity as Perfect Becky to God and be content being just Becky.

Part of this process has been making the choice to include more leisure in my life, more time where I do something that I want to do, just because I want to do it. I might sit and do a craft or sewing project. I might sit and watch a movie or talk to a friend. As I've been making those choices, I've also had to repent of the judgments I place on myself for taking time for me or taking time to

do nothing rather than be productive or be serving other people. I've had to reframe my thinking about rest and accept that it is a godly activity.

It is getting easier for me to make choices that show more honor to myself. What is interesting is the many positive ways that slowing down is impacting my life. I am more connected to God than I ever have been. I don't worry about whether God is pleased with me because I can feel open to receiving God's love. I am still successful in my career, with less stress and worry. I still serve other people, but I feel like the service I am choosing to do is more meaningful and joyful for me and more impactful on other people. I feel more peaceful and content with my life. I have enjoyed slowing down and learning to rest in God.

Make time for rest, both on a daily and weekly basis. As you rest, stay in balance with God. Choose to use that time to receive from God. You can even tell God that your intention is to receive from Him. Tell Him what you need. If you are feeling physically weak, then ask for strength. If you feel emotionally frazzled, then ask for peace. If your mind is worn out, then ask for help being present and stilling your mind. God *delights* in blessing you. When you use your agency to choose to receive God's gifts, then you will be blessed beyond measure.

Learning to rest in God is a beautiful process. As you rest in God and your capacity to receive from Him expands, you will change and grow. The whole process elevates you.

Through learning to rest, you are teaching yourself how to come into God's presence. As you receive more of your hopes from God, you will feel complete and whole. That feeling of having everything you desire will elevate your desires even more. Your hopes will bring you closer and closer to God. By resting and expanding your capacity to receive from God, you will one day receive the ultimate hope that you can receive in this life—to be in the presence of God and to feel His love for you.

# Chapter 12
## Putting It All Into Practice

We hope that you feel excited and energized by the information in this book. We hope you are eager to use hope, faith, and charity to work with God to create a life you love. This journey takes effort, and it is a process. Starting this journey can be especially challenging because it takes so much faith to start creating your hope without any tangible evidence that your efforts will pay off. As with any journey, you will hit unexpected challenges that might make you feel the process does not work or that you are doing it wrong. In this chapter, we discuss some insights to help you on this journey.

First, remember that your primary responsibility and your primary focus through this whole journey is staying in balance with God. If you get overwhelmed by the process or feel doubt about whether it is working, then you have fallen out of balance with God. No matter where you are in the process, stay focused on your balance. God can calm your overwhelmed state and give you greater understanding. God desires to reassure you when you feel

discouraged, but you will only feel that reassurance when you have gotten back into balance. By staying in balance, you will be more open to God's inspiration and direction about what to do next. No matter what is going on, focus on staying in balance.

Second, stay aware of your thoughts and feelings about the process itself because there will be times when you might have a strong emotional reaction to it. You might feel overwhelmed by all of this information. You might feel confused or even afraid that the information is wrong. You might doubt whether it will work. You might be afraid that it will not work for you or discouraged about how difficult it is to stay in balance. You might worry that you are doing something wrong. You might feel that you are not doing as well at receiving your hopes as those around you are and feel jealous and discouraged. You might worry what other people will think of you. Stay aware of these thoughts, emotions, and judgments. Repent of them. Forgive yourself and forgive your feelings. Forgive the process for being hard or confusing or for taking too long. Surrender all of these feelings to God through the repentance process and focus on staying in balance. It is natural and normal to stumble along the way. When that happens, forgive yourself and get back into balance.

Third, remember that your emotions are your friends in this process, not your enemies. Even your undesirable emotions are helping you with your creations. Just because you feel anger or fear or discouragement, it does not mean that this process is not working. In reality, those emotions will speed up the creation process by acting as neon signs pointing out the next thing in your life that needs attention, such as a limiting belief or a past

experience that needs to be healed. When you feel any undesirable emotion, such as fear, take a few minutes to reflect on your thoughts and emotions. When you have identified what you are thinking and feeling, then forgive those thoughts and emotions and surrender them to God through the repentance process. Embrace your emotions as they come up and be grateful for what they are teaching you. Your emotions will help you to see those things in your life that require more repentance and forgiveness.

Everything in your life is designed to help you on this journey, even painful and difficult experiences. Your mortal mind will be tempted to interpret obstacles, difficulties, and roadblocks as a sign that you are doing something wrong or that the process is not working. However, these obstacles and challenges are actually perfectly designed opportunities to bring the healing necessary for you to receive your creations. These experiences will show you the emotions and limiting beliefs that are preventing you from receiving your hopes. As these experiences arise, repent of them. Repent of all of the beliefs and emotions associated with that particular challenge or experience. Forgive yourself, your challenges, and your thoughts and feelings. Apply the tools in this book to every road bump in your way. Retrain your mind to view your experiences as a gift to help you create what you desire. Without any road bumps, you will never see those things in your life that are preventing you from receiving your creation.

Finally, you may reach a point where you are so discouraged with the process that you want to quit. You might feel that you just cannot do it any longer and that you are ready to give up. *That is wonderful!* When you get to that point, it means that you are on the verge of a breakthrough

that will upgrade your ability to receive your creation from God. Instead of quitting, apply your tools of forgiveness and repentance to all your frustrations and your desire to quit. As you repent, express all of your frustration and anger to God. When you have fully vented all of your feelings, forgiven them, and repented of them, you will be elevated to a state of peace and joy that was greater than what you had been experiencing prior to starting the creation process. Your moment of crisis precipitated a huge breakthrough that enlarged your capacity to receive joy and peace and purified energy from God. Know that these moments of crisis will come and that they are part of the process. Just keep going because something beautiful is on the other side.

## How Do You Know It Is Working?

One of the most challenging things about creation is that it takes some time before you receive your creation. This means that it takes time before you have tangible evidence that hope, faith, and charity are working. This is why it is a journey of faith; you have to maintain hope in your creation even without evidence that it is coming to you. Many people desire some kind of feedback or sign that what they are doing is working.

One way to see the evidence that this process is working in your life is to use the process in chapter 9 to assess your faith. Rate yourself on a scale of 1 to 10 for (a) how much you believe in your capacity to stay balanced and receive your creation, (b) God's ability to deliver your creation to you, and (c) your belief that your creation is possible. After you do your ratings, forgive yourself for scoring anything less than a 10 in any area. Repent of each of these assessments, surrender them to God, and

get back into balance. Then, for the next week, focus only on staying in balance throughout the day. At the end of the week, rate your faith again in those three areas. You will likely see some improvement in your self-ratings— and that is a victory. Over time, you will see all of those numbers increase. Use that to bolster your faith in the creation process. When you can honestly rate yourself as a "10" in all three areas, then sit back and choose to receive your creation into your life. It will not take long for it to happen.

If your self-rating does not improve at all, that is an opportunity for more repentance and forgiveness. Forgive your faith for not growing. Forgive yourself for stagnating. Forgive your creation for not appearing. Forgive the process. Repent of your self-ratings and how you feel about them. Spend some time repenting and surrender all of the emotions and beliefs you have about your faith to Jesus Christ. After you do so, your faith scores will naturally increase. Remember that faith, like hope and charity, is a gift from God. Pray for this gift.

Another way to know that this process is working is to pay attention to your life and how you feel. You might not receive all of your creations right away, but ask yourself the following questions:

- Is your life improving in other small ways?

- Are things getting easier?

- Are you feeling happier?

- Do you feel closer to God?

- Are you learning more quickly?

- Is it getting easier to stay in balance?

- Are you having positive experiences with repentance and forgiveness?

- Do you have more peaceful moments?

The process of hope, faith, and charity will make your life better and happier in many ways. If you pay attention, you will see your life shift positively in many small ways. It means that the process is working because it is changing you!

The process is also working if you can feel your relationship with God changing. The creation process only works if you put your trust in God and use His power and not just your own power. It only works if you repent frequently and allow God to heal and change you. You can only create your desires if you are balanced and connected to God throughout the day. The wonderful thing is that focusing on God and accessing God's power strengthens and develops your relationship with God. You will feel more and more that God is part of your life. You will feel God's love for you. You will feel closer to God and have more guidance and inspiration.

## This Is a Process of Becoming

The great beauty of hope, faith, and charity is that they can change you. Do not get discouraged if you have not received your hope yet. The process itself and how it changes you are really the most important things, not necessarily receiving a specific hope in a specific time frame. People often want to use these creation tools to escape from challenging situations in their lives, which means that as long as that challenging situation remains, they will be frustrated and discouraged. While your hope to escape a challenging situation is normal and understandable,

God's design for your life is much bigger than that specific hope. His design is for you to be fundamentally changed through the process—to have your hope, faith, and charity grow. Your spirit desires to go through this process for the growth that it offers and not just to receive one or two specific hopes, however precious they may be. This is a process of becoming, a process of change.

If you are trying to use these creation tools to escape a problem or negative situation in your life, then you have a strong emotional attachment to your hope. Remember that attachment to your hope means that you are depending on that hope for your happiness. If you get discouraged that you are not receiving your hope, that is evidence that you are afraid you will not receive that hope. Repent of that attachment and surrender it to God. Allow God to dissolve your attachment and replace it with peace and contentment. Your attachment is one of the things preventing you from receiving your hope because it is an indication of your past wounds and unhealed emotions. Pray for the desire to be happy without ever receiving this hope. The more you let go of your attachment to your hope, the more you open yourself up to receive it. God can change your heart for you and elevate you to a state where you feel completely happy and peaceful whether or not you receive your hope. This is part of how God changes you in this process.

Instead of continually looking to see if your hopes have arrived in your life, focus on having joy in the process itself. Take pleasure in the fact that you are being changed as you exercise hope, faith, and charity. Be happy when you see it become easier and easier for you to stay balanced. Learn to love every aspect of the process and to

savor each moment that brings you closer to your hopes. When you fall in love with the process, the results will follow. That state of peace and contentment is an indication that you are in balance and that God's power is working on your behalf. Staying in balance most of the time is a huge victory.

Hope, faith, and charity are essential in your progress toward godhood. These tools help you to master your own agency because using these tools means that you must be aware of and intentional about the choices you are making each moment. Choosing balance in every moment requires dedicated application of your agency. As you repent, everything in your life will be elevated. As you rest in God, your ability to receive God's power in your life will be enhanced. Faith, hope, and charity are God's recipe for you to master your agency and progress in the most gentle and efficient way possible. Mastered agency is what qualifies you for godhood because mastered agency opens the floodgates of God's grace.

The counterfeit recipe is knowledge, expectations, and judgment. In this recipe, you must do everything on your own instead of relying on God's power. While this recipe can help you to accomplish many of your goals and achieve status and power, it does not help you to progress toward godhood. In fact, it limits your ability to create and limits your use of your agency. When you are working from your own knowledge, you are limiting the amount of power that God can bring into your life and the miracles that manifest. Your expectations are grounded in your fears, so they often lead you to greater worry and anxiety. Expectations can also set you up for big disappointments, which can bring up your harshest judgments. Those judgments will

lock into place every negative thing in your life. Judgment will imprison you in a life that you hate.

Hope, faith, and charity, on the other hand, will free you. They will unshackle you from pain, lack, and struggle. It will take some work and effort to learn how to master these three eternal principles. Keep hoping, repenting, forgiving, and walking in faith. Maintain your balance with God every day. Keep choosing the life that you desire. You *will* get better at this. It *will* become easier. You *will* see and feel your own progress. You *will* see your relationship with God grow. Make a commitment to yourself right now that you will continue to walk this journey of faith and keep partnering with God in every moment, even when you encounter obstacles. Determine that you will keep practicing every day until you are once again living in the presence of God.

## Conclusion

The purpose of this book is to provide you with greater understanding about how to use your agency and power to create a more wonderful, more beautiful life. It is possible to do this. While opposition is a necessary condition of mortality, you are not restricted to learning and growth through pain and sorrow. You can choose to learn through joy instead of pain. There is a common saying that people attribute to Jesus Christ—"I never said it would be easy, I only said it would be worth it." That is actually a false statement. Christ *did* say that life could be easy.

*"Come unto me, all ye that labour and are heavy laden, and I will give you rest. Take my yoke upon you, and learn of me; for I am meek and lowly in heart: and ye shall find rest unto your souls. For*

*my yoke is easy, and my burden is light"* (Matthew
*11:38–30).*

God desires to carry your burdens for you and solve
your problems with you. God desires to bless you with all of
the desires of your heart. While many people believe this,
they often believe that it will not come until some far off,
distant day. That is not true. *The easy yoke that Christ offers
you is something that you can have right now.* Every moment
that you choose to be balanced is a moment where God is
fully shouldering your burdens. You can choose that again
and again, moment after moment. The more you put your
trust in hope, faith, and charity, the more you will see miracles arrive in your life on a daily basis. You will be happy
and content with your life and filled with gratitude for
what you are receiving. Your life will be filled with more
ease. You will experience a beautiful mastery of yourself
that will draw you into God's presence and fill you with
joy.

# About the Authors

*Lacey Bangerter* grew up in a family of ten children in American Fork, Utah. Being homeschooled for a good portion of her life she became open minded to alternative learning and disciplined in being self-taught. In 2007, she served a full time mission for the church of Jesus Christ of Latter Day Saints in New Jersey and has been an active member of the Church her whole life. She is married and has four children and lives with her family in Eagle Mountain, Utah. Her unique life experiences from beyond the veil led her to become the creator of "My Perfect Balance" living, a therapist, a podcaster, teacher and speaker. She is thrilled to add author to that list as she presents the book, *Awaking the God Within*, with her co-author Rebecca Nesbit.

*Rebecca Nesbit* is a teacher, speaker, and writer. She is an avid devotee of personal growth and development and is delighted to debut *Awaking the God Within* as her first book in the genre. Rebecca is a proud resident of Athens, Georgia where she teaches at the University of Georgia (go dawgs!). She lives with a confident cat, a shy cat, a talkative cat, and an endearing dog.

We would love to hear about the amazing things you have created in your life using the information in this book.

Please share your stories with us at:

OWL IN THE
juniper

owlinthejuniperpublishing@gmail.com